· TRADITIONAL ·
Jewish Baking

· TRADITIONAL ·
Jewish Baking

RETRO RECIPES YOUR GRANDMA WOULD MAKE...
IF SHE HAD A MIXER

· CARINE GOREN ·

AUTHOR OF *SWEET SECRETS, SWEET SECRETS 2* AND *BAKING IS CHILD'S PLAY*
AND HOST OF ISRAEL'S TOP BAKING SHOW

PAGE STREET
PUBLISHING CO.

PAGE STREET
PUBLISHING CO.

Copyright © 2016 Carine Goren

Originally published in Israel "im lesauta haya mixer" © 2013 Cookie Media LTD

Published in 2016 by
Page Street Publishing Co.
27 Congress Street, Suite 103
Salem, MA 01970
www.pagestreetpublishing.com

Distributed by Macmillan, sales in Canada by The Canadian Manda Group.

19   18   17   16   1   2   3   4   5

ISBN-13: 9781624142796
ISBN-10: 1624142796

Library of Congress Control Number: 2016906044

Cover and book design by Page Street Publishing Co.
English translation by Hanna Ben Tzvi-Goren
Culinary Editor: Moran Amrami Rozenboim
Photography by Daniel Lailah

Printed and bound in China

Page Street is proud to be a member of 1% for the Planet. Members donate one percent of their sales to one or more of the over 1,500 environmental and sustainability charities across the globe who participate in this program.

To Nicole and Michael (a.k.a. Mom and Dad),
When God made parents, He gave me the best ones.

Contents

Introduction

These days, grandmothers look just as fabulous as their daughters; 60 is the new 40, and gray hair and wrinkles seem like a faraway fiction. The past few decades have definitely been revolutionary.

Grandmas are not the only ones undergoing change. Our kitchens are unrecognizable. Larger than ever, they are equipped with cutting-edge baking ovens, microwave ovens and mixers. The sophisticated tools and gadgets available to baking connoisseurs nowadays would put any bakery to shame. The pompous, female-oriented cookbooks of 40 years ago have been replaced by the appealing and user-friendly publications of our day, featuring scrumptious pictures and clear instructions addressed to all genders. Each home boasts at least one shelf of colorful cookbooks, and I haven't even mentioned the Internet yet . . .

The whole family has joined the (new) grandmothers in the kitchen. Interest in baking recognizes no age, status or ethnicity, and the once drudge position of "chef" has become a highly coveted, prestigious profession.

However, all those fancy and sophisticated macaroons and cupcakes pushed aside the recipes of yesterday: grandma's cakes and cookies that we all love and cherish. These recipes are timeless, from the fragrant yeast roulades to the tall—so very tall—lekach (torte) cakes, the simple, melt-in-your-mouth cookies and the fluffy cheesecakes, not to mention grandma's more time-consuming and labor-intensive cakes (almost always boasting both crumble and meringue). And who can forget homemade candy?

In the past three years, I have been collecting, researching, experimenting and adapting thousands of grandma's recipes, until I was satisfied that I was holding in my hands (and my heart) the best of the best.

And then the real work began:

- Getting the precise measurements—not "by the eye" or "as it feels."

- Adapting old recipes to today's kitchen appliances, like the microwave oven and the stand mixer.

- Writing down every stage, not skipping any detail (not even "obvious" things safely stored in grandma's memory that did not require mentioning, let alone explaining).

- Upgrading some of the flavors—with the greatest respect for the original, of course—to correspond with modern tastes (the memory of the cake sometimes tastes better than the cake itself—you all know what I am talking about).

- Adding to many of the recipes a sweet little secret (dubbed in this book "Grandma Knows Best"), providing something extra, because, let's face it—grandmothers are not always generous with their knowledge.

So, what did I take from all this?

First and foremost, a healthy respect for grandma's recipes—it is the simplest ones that require the hands-on guidance and stand up anyone who never had a tall lekach sink like a flat tortilla!

Our grandmothers and our parents' grandmothers have dedicated their lives to lovingly cooking for and feeding their families, gaining wisdom and outstanding skill that professional chefs take years to achieve. For example, did you know that in order to prepare a "simple" Bavarian cream, one must cook a yolk-based crème Anglaise, dissolve gelatin, prepare whipped cream (not too stiff and not too soft, mind you), whip up an egg white meringue and fold it all together into a fluffy cream? Sounds complicated and daunting, doesn't it? Let me give you my own grandma's timeless pearl of wisdom: "First of all, calm down!"

True, acquiring these skills takes time, but if you let me hold your hand, we will master these nostalgic recipes step-by-step. With my detailed explanations and sweet little secrets accompanying them, anyone can do it!

Flavors from the past, so I have learned in the process, go straight to the heart.

This book is your chance to succumb to nostalgia, to excite relatives and to get acquainted—or reacquainted—with old recipes that, like us, have come from different places on the globe.

Now to my most important conclusion: A new generation of young bakers is literally growing under our aprons, and if we don't pass on the recipes of former generations, they may not even know what they would be missing. So I invite you to enjoy the tried and tested recipes in this book; they are the essence of my own journey down memory lane, and I hope that they give you the inspiration and motivation to collect and write down your own family recipes.

With all my love,

Carine Goren

THE CRÈME DE LA CRÈME

Nostalgic creamy desserts and whipped cream cakes—to me they are the best reason for having teaspoons in the house!

Black Forest Cake

Decadent, impressive and gorgeous, the Black Forest cake was the most festive creation in old-day confectionary shops (I dare you to wrap your tongues around its German name—Schwarzwälder kirschtorte). My version is a moist chocolate cake (a torte would be drier), with layers of whipped cream and cherries, and the most important thing—as corny as possible—with whipped cream roses, chocolate garnish and, of course, candied cherries. In my opinion, if you put in the time and effort to make such a cake, then you might as well go all out!

ONE 9-INCH (23-CM) CAKE

FOR THE CHOCOLATE CAKE

2 eggs

½ cup (120ml) vegetable oil

1 cup (240ml) buttermilk

1 cup (240ml) water

2 cups (400g) sugar

¾ cup (100g) cocoa

½ tsp salt

2 cups (280g) all-purpose flour

2 tsp (8g) baking powder

1 tsp baking soda

FOR THE CHERRIES AND SYRUP

1 (24-oz [680-g]) jar cherries in light syrup

Kirsch liquor or sweet wine (optional)

FOR THE WHIPPED CREAM FILLING AND GARNISH

3 cups (750ml) whipping cream

½ cup (100g) sugar

3 tbsp (30g) vanilla-flavored instant pudding mix

6 oz (150g) dark chocolate, divided

12 candied cherries

GRANDMA KNOWS BEST

You can make buttermilk at home; it's very easy. Mix 1 cup (240ml) of milk with a teaspoon of vinegar, set aside for 10 minutes and—hey, presto—homemade buttermilk!

To make the cake, preheat the oven to 325°F (160°C). Line two 9-inch (23-cm) pans with circles of parchment paper and grease the paper.

In a mixer on low speed, beat the eggs, oil, buttermilk, water, sugar, cocoa and salt for about 1 minute, until fully combined. Add the flour, baking powder and baking soda, and beat for another minute, until the batter is smooth and a little runny.

Pour the batter into the prepared pans, and bake for 40 minutes, until a toothpick inserted into the center comes out with moist crumbs. Remove from the oven and let cool completely. Slice each cake in half horizontally so you have 4 layers.

To prepare the cherries, strain the canned cherries, and save the syrup to moisten the cake. You may add a little Kirsch liquor or sweet wine to the syrup. Check for pits; you don't want any in the cake.

To make the whipped cream, in a mixer, beat together the whipping cream, sugar and pudding mix to a firm whipped cream. Spoon about a quarter of the whipped cream into a piping bag with a serrated tip and keep in the refrigerator (to decorate the cake later on).

Place one layer of cake on a serving platter, brush with the syrup, and spread an even layer of whipped cream. Spread one-third of the cherries over the cream. Put a second layer of cake on top, brush with syrup, spread an even layer of whipped cream and spread a handful of cherries. Repeat the layers one more time. Put the fourth and last layer of cake on top, and cover the whole assembly with the rest of the whipped cream.

In a microwave oven, melt 4 ounces (100g) of the chocolate. Put the melted chocolate in a small piping bag (or use a sandwich bag and cut the tip off).

On a parchment-lined baking tray, pipe crisscross lines of the melted chocolate, creating little chocolate "meshes" slightly taller than the cake itself. Put in the freezer for 5 minutes to set.

Use the cream you put in a piping bag earlier to pipe 12 roses on top of the cake, and put a candied cherry on top of each rose. Stick the chocolate crisscross garnishes to the sides of the cake. With a vegetable peeler, make chocolate "curls" from the remaining 2 ounces (50g) chocolate, and pile them in the center. Keep in the refrigerator and serve cold.

(continued)

Place one layer of cake on a serving platter, brush with syrup, and spread with whipped cream. Spread a handful of cherries.

Put a second layer of cake on top, brush with syrup, spread an even layer of whipped cream and spread a handful of cherries.

Repeat the layers one more time, put the fourth layer on top, and frost the cake with the rest of the whipped cream.

Stick the chocolate crisscross garnishes to the sides of the cake.

Shulah's Upgraded Meringue Whipped Cream

I met my own private chef when we were seventeen. He was a cadet at the military boarding school in Haifa and I attended the adjacent Reali High School, so we were in the same class. During a break, we snuck into his room and he offered me a cake his mother had brought when she came to visit on Shabbat. It stuck in my memory as the best thing I had ever eaten in my life, probably because at that point, I was already head-over-heels . . .

This is a time-honored Hanna Shaulov recipe, upgraded and upgraded again by my mother-in-law, substituting the margarine with butter, store-bought syrup with homemade chocolate ganache and so on. This cake is best prepared and assembled a day ahead, because it improves after a night in the refrigerator.

ONE 13 X 11-INCH (33 X 28-CM) CAKE

FOR THE CRUST
2 cups (280g) all-purpose flour

1 tsp baking powder

½ cup (100g) sugar

7 oz (200g) cold butter, diced

4 egg yolks (save the whites for the meringue)

FOR THE MERINGUE
4 egg whites

1 cup (200g) sugar

FOR THE COFFEE-FLAVORED WHIPPED CREAM FILLING
2 cups (480ml) whipping cream

½ cup (100g) sugar

1 tbsp (8g) instant coffee powder

FOR THE GARNISH
1 oz (30g) dark chocolate

2 tbsp (30ml) whipping cream

To make the crust, preheat the oven to 350°F (180°C). Line a 13 x 11-inch (33 x 28-cm) cake pan with parchment paper.

In a food processor, mix together the flour, baking powder, sugar and butter cubes to a flaky consistency. Add the yolks, and mix only until a ball of dough is formed. Press the dough into the prepared pan and bake for about 20 minutes, until the crust has risen, is golden and is baked all the way through. Set aside to cool.

To make the meringue, lower the oven temperature to 250°F (120°C).

In a mixer, beat the egg whites at medium speed for 1 minute, until a white froth with large bubbles forms. Gradually, add the sugar and beat until stiff and shiny.

On a sheet of parchment paper, draw a rectangle the size of the baking pan. Place the parchment sheet face down (so the ink doesn't touch the meringue) on a baking sheet. Spread all of the meringue in a thick layer within the lines marked on the parchment sheet. Bake for 3 hours, until the meringue is dry to the touch, beginning to turn gold and easily comes off the paper. Set aside until completely cool.

Right before assembly, make the coffee whipped cream filling. In a mixer, beat together the whipping cream, sugar and instant coffee, until thick and firm. Spread the whipped cream on the baked base, cover with the meringue and press down carefully.

To make the garnish, in a microwave oven, heat the chocolate and whipping cream until melted through, and whisk together to get a smooth sauce. Decorate the meringue by drizzling with the chocolate sauce.

Keep in the refrigerator for 2–3 hours (preferably overnight) before serving. Serve cold.

GRANDMA KNOWS BEST

If you don't have an extra 2 tablespoons (30ml) whipping cream for the chocolate sauce, you can "steal" 2 tablespoons (30ml) from the filling (or simply mix the melted chocolate with a teaspoon of oil to make it thinner).

Israeli Cremeschnitte (Napoleon Cake)

Not to be confused with the delicate Parisian mille-feuille (French for "a thousand leaves"), the cremeschnitte (or Napoleon, as it is sometimes called) is its flaky sister from the 'hood. Whereas the mille-feuille has thin, dense layers of pastry, baked under the weight of another baking tray, the cremeschnitte has thick, fluffy layers of puff pastry, and its only garnish is tons of powdered sugar on top. The European variety was originally made with a single layer of filling between two sheets of pastry; however, in Israel, another layer was added for a more impressive result.

ONE 14-INCH (35.5-CM) CAKE (8 SERVINGS)

FOR THE CRÈME PÂTISSIÈRE

2 cups (480ml) milk

1 tsp vanilla extract

4 egg yolks

¼ cup (40g) cornstarch

½ cup (100g) granulated sugar

FOR THE PUFF PASTRY LAYERS

1 lb (450g) frozen, pre-rolled puff pastry, defrosted

About 1 cup (200g) granulated sugar, for sprinkling

FOR THE WHIPPED CREAM

2 tbsp (25g) granulated sugar

1 cup (240ml) whipping cream

FOR THE GARNISH

Powdered sugar

GRANDMA KNOWS BEST

A famous French pastry chef once told me that they prepare the mille-feuille four times a day in their pâtisserie, because it must be super-fresh. I don't think we must be so fussy; however, it is recommended to prepare this cake on the day of serving or one day ahead at the most, because the puff pastry quickly absorbs moisture from the filling and from the refrigerator, and it softens.

To make the crème pâtissière, begin at least 4 hours before you plan to serve, to allow time for cooling and setting. In a large pot over medium-high heat, heat the milk and vanilla until almost boiling. At the same time, in a bowl, whisk together the egg yolks, cornstarch and granulated sugar to a light, creamy consistency. Pour a ladle of the hot milk into the yolk mixture, and whisk quickly. Transfer the yolk mixture back to the pot with the hot milk, and heat again over medium heat, whisking constantly, until the first bubbles appear (it should look like porridge).

Remove from the heat, pour into a clean bowl and immediately cover with plastic wrap (the plastic should cling to the cream to prevent a skin from forming). Let cool and then put in the refrigerator for at least 4 hours, until the cream is very cold and set.

To make the puff pastry layers, preheat the oven to 350°F (180°C). Generously sprinkle the granulated sugar over your work surface, and lay down the pastry sheet. Sprinkle some more sugar on the pastry sheet, and roll with a rolling pin just a little to make the sugar stick, and to get a slightly thinner sheet of pastry (about ¼-inch [6-mm] thick). Cut the pastry sheet into 3 long and narrow rectangles. Transfer the pastry rectangles to baking trays lined with parchment paper, and poke with a fork. Bake for approximately 20 minutes, until golden and very fluffy. Let cool completely.

Use an empty (and clean) baking tray to gently press down on the baked pastry sheets to flatten and achieve an even thickness. Turn the pastry sheets upside down (crumbs will fall, but that's okay). The edges may have twisted slightly during baking. If you want a straight and symmetrical result, use a serrated bread knife to trim about ¼ inch (6mm) off each side.

To make the whipped cream, in a mixer, beat the sugar and cream to a very firm whipped cream. Transfer the whipped cream to another large bowl. In the mixer bowl (no need to wash it), put the now chilled and solid crème pâtissière. Beat at high speed for 1 minute, until the crème pâtissière regains its smooth and creamy consistency. Add the crème pâtissière to the whipped cream in the big bowl, and gently fold them together with a rubber spatula.

To assemble the cake, lay the first pastry rectangle on a platter and spread (or pipe) half of the whipping cream mixture on top. Lay another rectangle on the cream and press down lightly. Spread or pipe the rest of the cream. Cut the third rectangle into smaller squares (the size of an individual portion), and lay them close together on top (this will make cutting the cake easier). Place in the refrigerator for 1 hour, so the filling will set. This ensures smooth and precise slicing. Slice and sprinkle with the powdered sugar for garnish.

Bavarian Cream

Bavarian cream needs a lot of work and TLC; the vanilla cream must be cooked, the gelatin dissolved and the whipping cream and egg whites whipped (separately). Then they all must be folded together and set aside to cool for 4 hours. However, it is sooo worth it! This dessert will take you smiling down memory lane and fill you with sweet nostalgia. The Israeli steakhouse Bavaria of yesteryear had always been nondairy. This recipe, however, is a rich and creamy version that is sweeter than those memories. If you are put off by the raw eggs, let me refer you to page 22, where you will find another recipe (the "cheat") without eggs, which is also great.

ONE 13 X 11-INCH (33 X 28-CM) PAN

FOR THE GELATIN MIXTURE
1 oz (28g) gelatin powder
1 tbsp (12g) sugar
½ cup (120ml) water

FOR THE WHIPPED CREAM
2 cups (480ml) whipping cream

FOR THE VANILLA CREAM
6 egg yolks (save the whites for the meringue)
2 tbsp (20g) cornstarch
¾ cup (150g) sugar
1 tbsp (15ml) vanilla extract
2 cups (480ml) milk

FOR THE MERINGUE
6 egg whites
½ cup (100g) sugar

FOR SERVING
Chocolate syrup
Chopped walnuts

To make the gelatin mixture, combine the gelatin powder with the sugar. Pour the water into a bowl, sprinkle the gelatin and sugar mix over the water and set aside to dissolve.

To make the whipped cream, in a mixer, beat the whipping cream to soft peaks. Transfer to a clean bowl and put in the refrigerator (do not clean the mixer bowl or the whisk attachment—use them right away for the vanilla cream).

To make the vanilla cream, in a small pan (not yet on the stove), combine the egg yolks, cornstarch, sugar and vanilla and whisk vigorously for 1 minute, until the mixture lightens. Add the milk, and continue to whisk until combined. Put the pot on the stove over medium heat and continue whisking until the mixture thickens and begins to boil. When the first bubbles appear, take the pot off the heat, and immediately pour the egg yolk mixture into the mixer bowl. Beat at high speed for 5 minutes, until the vanilla cream cools to room temperature (it won't rise or froth; it will just cool).

In a microwave oven, heat the gelatin until it melts, about 20 seconds (take care not to boil). Add it to the vanilla cream, and beat until incorporated. Pour the cream into a clean bowl and set aside.

To make the meringue, thoroughly clean the mixer bowl and whisk. In the clean mixer bowl, beat the egg whites at medium speed until a soft white froth forms. With the mixer still on medium speed, gradually add the sugar, a spoonful at a time, waiting 10 seconds between spoonfuls. After all of the sugar has been incorporated, continue to beat for another 2 minutes.

Add the vanilla cream to the meringue in the mixer bowl, and beat together at low speed until incorporated. Add the whipped cream and, again, beat until incorporated. Pour the batter into an oiled 13 x 11-inch (33 x 28-cm) pan, and put in the refrigerator for 4 hours before serving.

To serve, cut into small squares, decorate with the chocolate syrup and garnish with the chopped walnuts. Serve cold. Keep any extra in the refrigerator.

"Bavarian Cheat" (without eggs)

Thanks to this version, I could treat my pregnant sister (and the unborn Emma) to Bavarian cream.

MAKES ONE 13 X 11-INCH (33 X 28-CM) PAN

2 cups (480ml) milk

1 oz (28g) gelatin

1 cup (200g) sugar

3 cups (750g) prepared vanilla-flavored pudding

1 cup (250g) cream cheese

1 cup (250g) Greek yogurt

2 cups (480ml) whipping cream

Pour the milk into a pot, sprinkle the gelatin over the milk, and set aside to dissolve.

In a bowl, combine the sugar, pudding, cream cheese and yogurt. Set aside for 5 minutes, until the sugar is completely dissolved.

Over medium heat, heat the milk and gelatin mixture while stirring, until the gelatin has melted and the milk is hot (make sure it doesn't boil). Add all of the hot milk and gelatin mixture to the pudding and cheese mixture, and whisk until smooth.

In a mixer, beat the whipping cream to soft peaks, add to the cheese mixture and stir until combined. Pour into a 13 x 11-inch (33 x 28-cm) pan, and cool for 4 hours before serving. Don't forget to decorate with chocolate syrup and chopped walnuts.

Easy No Yeast Family-Style Savarin

Well, this is not really a proper savarin—it is a simple sponge cake, soaked in syrup and topped with whipped cream. However, the moistness and flavor combination are reminiscent of the real thing.

ONE 9½-INCH (24-CM) ROUND CAKE

FOR THE CAKE
2 eggs

½ cup (100g) sugar

1 cup (240g) sour cream

1 cup (120g) all-purpose flour

1 tsp baking powder

1 cup (240ml) cold water

FOR THE SYRUP
1 cup (200g) sugar

1 cup (240ml) water

A few drops rum extract

FOR THE WHIPPED CREAM AND GARNISH
2 cups (480ml) whipping cream

5 tbsp (60g) sugar

2 tbsp (24g) vanilla-flavored instant pudding mix

16 candied cherries

Preheat the oven to 350°F (180°C) and grease a 9½-inch (24-cm) round pan.

To make the cake, in a bowl, whisk together the eggs, sugar, sour cream, flour and baking powder. Spread the batter in the prepared pan and bake until golden, about 20 minutes (the cake will come out low, and that's okay). Pour the cold water over the cake, and let cool completely.

To make the syrup, in a small pan, bring the sugar and water to a boil, add a few drops of rum extract and boil for 2 minutes. Moisten the cake with the syrup and cool a little.

To make the whipped cream, beat the whipping cream, sugar and pudding mix to stiff peaks, spread over the cake and garnish with the candied cherries. Chill in the refrigerator for 2 hours before serving.

GRANDMA KNOWS BEST

Have your savarins disintegrated? No biggie: it happens to the best of us, because the line between a perfectly soaked, solid savarin and one that "drank" too much is fine indeed. To minimize the risk, the soaking process must be slow, gradual and controlled, so I put the savarins in a hot but not boiling syrup. In the future, simply cut the soaking time short and everything will be fine. Ultimately, a less pretty but moist savarin is better than a perfect-looking dry one (and the whipped cream will hide any imperfections, anyway).

Soaked Savarins with Whipped Cream and a Cherry on Top

These are not the dainty French rum baba you may remember from my book *Sweet Secrets*. Here, each one is a "rum baba" to be reckoned with: big, moist, with a gaping "mouth" filled with whipped cream, and with a cherry—without which no rum baba or savarin is worthy of its name—perched proudly on top.

16 SAVARINS

FOR THE DOUGH
3 cups (420g) all-purpose flour
1 tbsp (8g) active dry yeast
3½ oz (100g) butter
1 cup (240ml) milk
4 eggs
½ cup (100g) sugar
¼ tsp salt

FOR THE SYRUP
5 cups (1.2L) water
2½ cups (500g) sugar
½ orange, sliced (with the peel)
1 tbsp (15ml) vanilla extract
1 tbsp (15ml) rum extract or
½ cup (120ml) real rum

FOR THE WHIPPED CREAM AND CHERRIES
2 cups (480ml) whipping cream
5 tbsp (60g) sugar
2 tbsp (20g) vanilla-flavored instant pudding mix
16 candied cherries, for garnish

To make the dough, in a stand mixer fitted with the kneading hook, combine the flour and yeast.

Melt the butter in a microwave oven. Add the milk and mix together to a lukewarm liquid mixture.

To the mixer bowl, add the eggs, sugar, salt and the butter and milk mixture, and knead at low speed for about 1 minute to incorporate. Knead for 5 more minutes at medium speed, to get a runny, sticky and shiny batter. Cover and set aside to rise until it doubles in bulk, 45–60 minutes.

Punch down or knead the dough to let out the air. Grease 16 cups of 2 muffin trays, and put a heaping spoon of batter in each cavity (up to half its height). Set aside to rise again, until doubled in bulk. Toward the end of this rising stage, preheat your oven to 375°F (190°C).

Bake for 15–20 minutes, until the savarins are golden brown and springy to the touch. Set aside to cool a little bit, and release from the pan.

To make the syrup, in a large, wide pot over medium heat, heat the water, sugar and orange slices until the sugar is dissolved. Bring to a boil, and continue cooking for another 2 minutes. Take off the heat, and add vanilla and rum extracts. Set aside 1 cup (240ml) of the syrup for serving.

Put 3 or 4 savarins (not more because they rise) into the remaining hot syrup, and soak for 2 minutes, until they begin to submerge in the syrup. Turn over, and leave in the syrup for another 5 minutes, until they are fluffed up, soaked through and heavy. Scoop the savarins out with a perforated spoon, and gently put them on a cooling tray. Repeat the soaking process with all the savarins (if the syrup has cooled, reheat and remove from the flame before resuming). Let the savarins cool completely.

To make the whipped cream, in a mixer, beat the whipping cream, sugar and instant pudding mix to stiff peaks. Transfer to a piping bag with a serrated (star-shaped) tip.

Place each savarin in a serving cup or small bowl, and pour a little of the reserved syrup over it. Slice about ½ inch (1.3cm) off the top of each savarin, almost all the way through, leaving the sliced top attached at one end. Carefully lift the top and pipe a tall pile of whipped cream under it. Put a candied cherry on top of the whipped cream pile, and serve. Store in the refrigerator.

Daddy Micha's Jerusalem Malabi

A sweet memory from my dad's childhood in Jerusalem, this dessert is usually served in a large Pyrex pan, cut into squares (like the Bavarian cream) and garnished with peanuts and lots of cinnamon. Slightly different from the recipe in my first book, *Sweet Secrets*, this malabi is thicker and firmer, so it maintains its shape when sliced (the preparation process here is also friendlier). Malabi can be served plain (snow-white), with the different toppings in separate bowls, but for my dad, I always take the trouble to decorate it with beautiful stripes on top.

ONE 14 X 8-INCH (35.5 X 20-CM) PAN

FOR THE MALABI
1½ cups (200g) cornstarch

1 cup (200g) sugar

1 tsp vanilla extract

8⅓ cups (2L) milk, divided

½ cup (120ml) rose water, or ½ cup (120ml) water with 1 tsp rose extract

2 cups (480ml) whipping cream

FOR THE GARNISH
1 cup (100g) roasted unsalted pistachio nuts or peanuts, chopped

1 cup (100g) desiccated coconut

2 tbsp (12g) ground cinnamon

½ cup (120g) raspberry concentrate

To make the malabi, in a big pot (not yet on the stove!), combine the cornstarch, sugar and vanilla. Add 2 cups (480ml) of the milk and whisk vigorously, until all lumps are dissolved. Add the remaining 6⅓ cups (1440ml) milk, rose water and whipping cream.

Place the pot over medium heat and bring to a boil, whisking constantly. As soon as the mixture begins to bubble, take the pot off the heat, and pour into a 14 x 8-inch (35.5 x 20-cm) Pyrex pan. Place plastic wrap directly on the malabi to prevent a skin from forming. Cool, and put in the refrigerator for at least 4 hours to set.

To garnish, just before serving, lightly (between three fingertips, like you would salt), sprinkle the chopped pistachio nuts and desiccated coconut in alternating diagonal lines. Sprinkle vertical lines of cinnamon over them (see photo). This dessert is best eaten straight out of the pan, but you can cut it into squares and serve with lots of raspberry concentrate.

GRANDMA KNOWS BEST
If the mixture almost reaches the boiling point, it will thicken all at once, and after cooling, the malabi will be very firm and easy to slice. If, however, the malabi did not reach the right temperature on the stove, it will be thinner and remain too soft even after cooling. In this case, the malabi can be poured into individual clear glasses and garnished.

Grandma Leonor's Flan

The most coveted dish at the Meiri clan's gatherings is Grandma Leonor's flan. Mind you, admitting that any dessert is better than barbecued beef is no small thing to an Argentine family. Leonor serves her flan in individual deep bowls, with a spoon of the caramel sauce and a heaped teaspoon of dulce de leche on the side. Sounds too sweet, right? Well, it's not, because the flan itself is only mildly sweet. To eat, spread some dulce de leche on the tip of your teaspoon, fill it with flan and a little bit of sauce and feast your heart out. So, forget the flan made from a mix. This here is the real McCoy—creamy, velvety and smooth on the tongue. A big thank-you to Leonor and her granddaughter, Einat Meiri (a talented designer and a dear friend), who managed to put her hands on the precise recipe, and who also brought me the pan, with a flan prepared especially for me by Leonor.

ONE 8¼-INCH (21.5-CM) BUNDT PAN

FOR THE CARAMEL
1 cup (200g) sugar
¼ cup (60ml) water

FOR THE FLAN
10 eggs
1 cup (200g) sugar
4 cups (1L) milk
1 tbsp (15ml) vanilla extract

Dulce de leche, for serving

GRANDMA KNOWS BEST

The water bath must be big and relatively deep (up to half the height of the flan pan). If your oven trays are not deep enough, use a wide, low pot with metal handles. Fill it with water, put it in the oven (on an oven tray, of course) and place the flan pan in it.

Some of the caramel will inevitably stick to the pan. For easy cleanup, pour boiling water into the pan, and let sit for 5 minutes.

To make the caramel, combine the sugar and water in a pan over high heat and cook, without stirring, until the bubbles begin to disappear and the syrup turns a golden caramel. Remove from the heat and immediately pour into an 8½-inch (21.5-cm) Bundt pan (be careful, it's very hot!). Jiggle the pan a little, so the caramel distributes evenly and coats the bottom and a little bit of the sides. Set aside for 10 minutes to cool and set up.

To make the flan, preheat the oven to 325°F (160°C). Place a deep pan in the oven and fill it to 2 inches (5cm) with boiling water (the flan pan will be put in the water bath).

In a big bowl, whisk together the eggs and sugar for 1–2 minutes to combine.

In a pot, heat the milk and vanilla until almost boiling, and remove from the heat. Ladle some of the hot milk into the egg mixture and stir immediately until combined. Repeat. After these 2 ladles, you may add the rest of the hot milk, constantly whisking, until the mixture is homogenous. Strain the mixture (optional, but highly recommended for a smooth result without any curdled egg pieces).

Pour the mixture onto the caramel, and put in the water bath in the oven (make sure no water gets into the flan itself). Bake for about 1 hour, until the flan is firm but wobbly, like Jell-O. To make sure the flan is cooked through, stick a knife in the middle—it should come out clean.

Take the flan out of the water bath (carefully!) and out of the oven, and set aside to cool completely. Put in the refrigerator overnight (during this time, the caramel at the bottom will melt and become a sauce).

When ready to serve, insert a knife between the flan and the sides of the pan, and pass it all around to release from the pan. Cover with a serving plate (with some depth, to hold the sauce), and turn over, so the plate is now on the bottom and the pan on top. Tap the pan several times with a spoon, until the flan and the sauce are released onto the plate. Take the pan off, and allow the caramel sauce to drizzle down. Serve immediately, with dulce de leche on the side.

Whipped Cream, Strawberry and Jell-O Sponge

Despite its basic flavors of whipped cream, strawberry and Jell-O, this nostalgic cake is loved by grown-ups and little 'uns alike and devoured in no time. Besides, look how pretty it is.

ONE 10-INCH (25-CM) CAKE

FOR THE SPONGE CAKE
6 eggs, separated, at room temperature
¾ cup (150g) sugar
½ cup (70g) all-purpose flour
¼ cup (40g) cornstarch
3½ tbsp (50g) melted butter, lukewarm

FOR THE SYRUP
½ cup (120ml) water
½ cup (100g) sugar
1 tbsp (15ml) brandy

FOR THE VANILLA WHIPPED CREAM
2 cups (480ml) whipping cream
¾ cup (180ml) milk
¼ cup (50g) sugar
½ cup (80g) vanilla-flavored instant pudding mix

FOR THE STRAWBERRIES IN JELL-O
15–20 fresh strawberries
1 cup (170g) strawberry-flavored Jell-O mix
2½ cups (600ml) boiling water

GRANDMA KNOWS BEST

The cake must be assembled out of the pan and directly on the serving plate, because it is frosted all around. To block any dripping of Jell-O, use a springform pan slightly smaller than the cake itself. For the Jell-O to be really firm, use a little less water than is called for in the package directions. The piped whipped cream garnish around will hide the difference in diameter between the cake and the Jell-O layer.

To make the sponge cake, preheat the oven to 350°F (180°C). Grease a 10-inch (25-cm) springform pan.

In a mixer, beat the egg whites at medium speed for 1 minute, until white froth with large bubbles forms. Gradually add the sugar, and go on beating to get a stiff and shiny meringue.

Lower the mixer speed to the minimum, add the yolks and mix until combined. Add the flour and cornstarch (sifting is recommended), and mix until all lumps are smooth and dissolved. Add the melted butter, and go on mixing for a few more seconds, until combined.

Spread the batter in the prepared pan, and bake for 35 minutes, until the cake is golden and a toothpick inserted in its center comes out dry. Let cool completely.

To make the syrup, in a pot, bring the water and sugar to a boil. Cook for another minute, and then remove from the heat. Mix in the brandy and set aside.

Release the sponge cake from the pan, and cut horizontally into 2 equal halves. Brush each one with half the syrup.

To make the vanilla whipped cream, in a mixer, beat the whipping cream, milk, sugar and pudding mix to firm peaks. Put 3 or 4 spoonfuls of the whipped cream in a piping bag with a serrated tip (to decorate around the Jell-O layer), and put in the refrigerator.

Put the first sponge layer on a serving plate, spread a generous layer of whipped cream on it (about a third), and cover with the other sponge layer. Spread the remaining whipped cream on the top and sides of the cake. Freeze for 1 hour to set.

For the strawberries in Jell-O, clean and slice (or cut in half) the strawberries, and arrange them on the cake.

Place the frame of a 9-inch (23-cm) springform pan around the cake (to keep the Jell-O from drizzling down the sides). Dissolve the Jell-O mix in the boiling water, and cool for 2 minutes. Carefully pour over the strawberries. Put in the refrigerator for 2 hours so the Jell-O will set.

Very gently, remove the springform frame. Pipe little drops or rosettes of whipped cream around the edges with the reserved whipped cream. Slice the cake with a sharp knife (wipe clean between slices) and serve. Keep covered in the refrigerator.

Cheese and Crumb Cake to Die For

This is a new take on the cheese and crumb cake recipe from my book *Sweet Secrets*. Of course, that cake is magnificent in its own right, but I have baked it again and again, changing and adjusting the recipe each time, depending on what was in the refrigerator that day. I finally realized that I had in my hands a new and improved version, with sour cream in the filling, twice as much instant pudding mix, a lot more crumbs and even more sugar (because, as it turned out, everyone wanted it slightly sweeter). So, here is a sophisticated yet humble-looking cake that tastes exactly like grandma's.

ONE 10-INCH (25-CM) CAKE

FOR THE CRUST AND THE CRUMBS

2 cups (280g) all-purpose flour

2 tsp (8g) baking powder

⅓ cup (70g) sugar

1 tsp vanilla extract

7 oz (200g) cold butter, diced

4 egg yolks

FOR THE CHEESE FILLING

2 cups (480ml) whipping cream

1 cup (200g) sugar

½ cup (80g) vanilla-flavored instant pudding mix

¾ cup (200ml) sour cream

1 cup (250g) cream cheese

1 cup (250g) Greek yogurt

To make the crust and crumbs, preheat the oven to 350°F (180°C). Grease a 10-inch (25-cm) springform pan.

In a food processor, process together the flour, baking powder, sugar, vanilla extract and butter cubes to a flaky mixture. Add the egg yolks and process in pulses, only until fine crumbs are formed.

Press half of the crumb mixture into the bottom of the prepared pan in an even layer. Press the other half of the mixture into another pan (the size doesn't matter) lined with parchment paper. This will be for the crumb topping. Put both pans in the oven and bake for about 20 minutes, until golden. Set aside to cool completely.

To make the filling, in a mixer, beat the whipping cream, sugar, pudding mix and sour cream until smooth and firm. Lower the speed, add the cream cheese and yogurt, and beat for a few more seconds, until combined.

Spread the cheese mixture over the cooled baked crust in the pan. With your hands, crumble the other pan of the baked crumb mixture over the cheese filling.

Put in the refrigerator for at least 4 hours to set. To serve, slice with a knife that is dipped in boiling water between slices.

GRANDMA KNOWS BEST

Good beating is what holds this cake (with a little help from the pudding mix), so how will you know when it's beaten enough? It's simple; just tip the bowl to one side. If the batter "travels" with this motion, it is not ready yet, and will need more beating. A well-beat batter will stay firmly in the bottom of the bowl, and we can be sure that the cake won't collapse without the support of the pan.

Upgraded Biscuit Cake

I was going to write that this is my mother's biscuit cake, but it's every mother's biscuit cake. In my childhood home, this cake was served on Shabbat, in the summer, waiting for us in the refrigerator when we came back all browned by the sun (it was allowed back then). On especially hot days, Ma would put it in the freezer in the morning, so by the time we ate it, it was a proper ice cream cake. I am well aware of the civilized convention of serving it sliced on a nice plate, but it is much better to spoon it straight from the pan. My mother's chocolate version is a great upgrading: it is very tall (seven layers, including the frosting), with chocolate-flavored biscuits and lots of chocolate ganache on top, just the way I like it.

ONE 13 X 11-INCH (33 X 28-CM) PAN

FOR THE VANILLA CREAM
2 cups (480ml) whipping cream

2 cups (480ml) milk

1 cup (160g) vanilla-flavored instant pudding mix

½ cup (125g) cream cheese

½ cup (125g) Greek yogurt

FOR THE BISCUITS
1 cup (240ml) milk

16 oz (500g) chocolate- or vanilla-flavored biscuits

FOR THE CHOCOLATE FROSTING
½ cup (125ml) whipping cream

4 oz (120g) dark chocolate

To make the vanilla cream, in a mixer, beat together the whipping cream, milk and pudding mix to firm peaks. Add the cream cheese and yogurt, and beat for a few more seconds, until combined.

To make the biscuits, pour the milk into a cup and quickly dip a third of the biscuits in the milk. Arrange tightly in the bottom of a 13 x 11-inch (33 x 28cm) pan. Spread with a third of the cream. Repeat 2 more times, to get alternating layers of milk-dipped biscuits and vanilla cream (the top layer is cream). Put in the freezer for half an hour (this way, the chocolate frosting will not melt the cream).

To make the frosting, in a microwave oven, heat the whipping cream and chocolate, and whisk to a smooth sauce. Let it cool a little, and pour over the cake.

Put the cake in the refrigerator for 2–3 hours before serving, so the filling will set and the biscuits will soften. Serve cold.

GRANDMA KNOWS BEST

Feel like diversifying a little? Here are some ideas for different flavors:

Choco-choco biscuit cake: Replace the vanilla pudding mix with a chocolate-flavored one, and add 2 tablespoons (40g) Nutella spread to the mixer bowl.

Halva biscuit cake: Add to the mixer bowl ½ cup (130g) halva spread, and instead of chocolate ganache, decorate with chopped halva.

Coffee biscuit cake: Add to the mixer bowl 1 tablespoon (12g) instant coffee. Wet the biscuits with lukewarm coffee (instant coffee and water, without milk or sugar).

Dulce de leche and white chocolate biscuit cake: Substitute the vanilla-flavored pudding mix with a dulce de leche one (or add 3 heaping tablespoons [50g] of dulce de leche to the original filling). Instead of the chocolate ganache, prepare a dulce de leche and white chocolate frosting by melting together 2 tablespoons (30g) dulce de leche with 5 ounces (150g) white chocolate and ¼ cup (60ml) whipping cream. Let it cool a little, and spread on the cake.

Light biscuit cake (without whipping cream): In a bowl, whisk 2 cups (480ml) skim milk with ¾ cup (120g) vanilla-flavored pudding mix and ½ cup (100g) sugar (or sugar substitute). Set aside for 5 minutes to thicken. Mix in 2 cups (500g) light cream cheese and 1 cup (250g) low-fat yogurt (the mixture will be runny, but that's okay; it will set in the refrigerator). Assemble in alternating layers of biscuits dipped in skim milk and filling. Instead of frosting the cake with a chocolate ganache, you can garnish it with curls of sugar-free chocolate.

Biscuit Pyramid

Long before fondant and sculptured cakes, the dessert repertoire was limited to sponge cakes shaped like butterflies, teddy bears, trains and numbers corresponding to the age of the birthday boy or girl. The pinnacle of cake design was this triangular cake—highly nostalgic and great for "straightening" the edges ("I'm not eating, just trimming . . ."). Explaining the process is detailed and more time-consuming than the actual preparation, but I want you to have a perfect result, so bear with me.

ONE LONG, FREESTYLE CAKE (8–10 SERVINGS)

FOR THE VANILLA FILLING

1 cup (240ml) whipping cream

¾ cup (180ml) milk

5 tbsp (60g) sugar

½ cup (80g) vanilla-flavored instant pudding mix

½ cup (125g) cream cheese

½ cup (125g) Greek yogurt

FOR THE BISCUITS

¾ cup (180ml) milk

About ¾ lb (350g) square biscuits

FOR THE CHOCOLATE FROSTING

½ cup (125ml) whipping cream

4 oz (120g) dark chocolate

1 tbsp (15ml) honey for extra shine (optional)

To make the vanilla filling, in a mixer, beat together the whipping cream, milk, sugar and pudding mix to firm peaks. Add the cream cheese and yogurt, and go on beating for a few more seconds, until combined.

Take out a long strip of aluminum foil and fold it in half to the size of a baking tray, and lay it on your work surface.

To make the biscuits, pour the milk into a cup. Dip the biscuits in the milk and arrange 3 tight rows of 5 or 6 biscuits each (depends on the size of the aluminum sheet) on the aluminum. Make sure the biscuits are crosswise; it is important for shaping the pyramid. Spread half of the filling evenly on the biscuits.

Repeat, only this time the biscuits in the central row must be crosswise, while the biscuits in the right and left rows should be lengthwise (leaving a little of the filling underneath exposed). The next layer of filling is put—in generous scoops—only on the middle row of biscuits.

Slide your hands under the right and left sides of the cake, lift and bring the edges together, so the right and left rows of biscuits meet in the center and—voilà—we have a pyramid! Fold the aluminum foil around the pyramid to tighten it (or you can hold the edges of the foil together with clothespins), and very gently take it to the freezer. Freeze for 1 hour to set.

To make the frosting, in a microwave oven, heat the whipping cream, chocolate and honey, if using, and whisk to a smooth sauce.

Open the aluminum foil, spoon the sauce over the cake, one spoonful at a time, and let it drizzle down until the entire pyramid is covered (the chocolate will spread on the foil, but that's okay).

Transfer the cake—with the aluminum foil—onto a long serving tray, tear the sides of the foil and gently pull them from under the cake. Put the cake in the refrigerator for 4 hours to absorb all the flavors and soften the biscuits.

With a sharp knife dipped in boiling water, cut thick triangular slices, about 1½ inches (3.8cm). Keep in the refrigerator and serve cold.

Biscuit Cake with a Strawberry Heart

When I make this cake for people, they immediately know how much I love them, and I don't even have to say anything; in the center of each slice "beats" a red strawberry heart (seen through the Jell-O). This is the easiest non-baking cheesecake. Make a cream and biscuit cake, decorate with halved strawberries cut into little hearts and cover with strawberry-flavored Jell-O. The only "headaches" are the freezing and cooling times: 2 hours in the freezer without the strawberries and Jell-O layer, so the boiling Jell-O won't melt the filling, and 1 hour in the refrigerator (the completed cake) for the Jell-O to set.

ONE 13 X 11-INCH (33 X 28-CM) PAN

FOR THE VANILLA CREAM
2 cups (480ml) whipping cream
½ cup (120ml) milk
½ cup (80g) vanilla-flavored instant pudding mix
½ cup (100g) sugar
½ cup (125g) cream cheese
½ cup (125g) Greek yogurt

FOR THE BISCUITS
¾ cup (180ml) milk
½ lb (250g) square biscuits

FOR THE STRAWBERRIES AND JELL-O LAYER
15–20 strawberries
1 cup (170g) strawberry-flavored Jell-O mix
3 cups (720ml) boiling water

To make the vanilla cream, in a mixer, beat together the whipping cream, milk, pudding mix, sugar, cream cheese and yogurt until firm and creamy.

To make the biscuits, pour the milk into a cup. Dip half of the biscuits in the milk and arrange tightly on the bottom of a 13 x 11-inch (33 x 28-cm) deep rectangular pan. Spread half of the cream filling on the layer of biscuits. Dip the remaining biscuits in milk and arrange on the cream, and spread the remaining cream over the biscuits. Freeze for 2 hours, to set.

To make the strawberries and Jell-O layer, cut the strawberries in half, lengthwise, and with a little heart-shaped cookie cutter cut each one into a heart (see photos below). Arrange the strawberry hearts on the cold cheese cream.

Dissolve the Jell-O in the boiling water, and set aside for 5 minutes to cool. Gently pour the Jell-O over the cheese and strawberries.

Put in the refrigerator for 1 hour to set. Slice into squares to serve.

GRANDMA KNOWS BEST
You can shape the strawberries with a knife (their natural shape is not far from it), but with a cookie cutter you get a more even and pretty result: cut the strawberry in half lengthwise, put it face down on the work surface and press the cookie cutter down on it. Any leftover pieces can go into a fruit salad or can be snacked on straight from the cutting board.

Use a little heart-shaped cookie cutter to cut small strawberry hearts.

Leftovers! Yummy!

Arrange the strawberry hearts on the cold cheese cream.

Whipped Cream and Sour Cream Kataifi Cake

Tasting like the old days, this cake features a creamy filling between two layers of browned, crispy and sweet kataifi noodles. I add chopped caramelized pecans that "peek" through the layers. You can eat this cake straight away, and the noodles would really crack loudly in your mouth, but I like it better after it has spent the night in the refrigerator and the noodles have softened a little.

ONE 13 X 11-INCH (33 X 28-CM) PAN

FOR THE KATAIFI BASE

1 lb (500g) kataifi noodles, defrosted

6 oz (200g) melted butter, lukewarm

¾ cup (100g) powdered sugar

FOR THE CREAM FILLING

2 cups (480ml) whipping cream

½ cup (80g) vanilla-flavored instant pudding mix

1⅔ cups (400ml) sour cream

5 tbsp (60g) granulated sugar

1½ cups (200g) chopped caramelized pecans

To make the kataifi base, preheat the oven to 325°F (160°C). Line two 13 x 11-inch (33 x 28-cm) deep baking pans with parchment paper.

Mix the kataifi noodles with the melted butter and powdered sugar (really "shampoo" them with it for complete and even coverage). Spread half of the kataifi noodles in each pan. Bake for 25–30 minutes, until golden. Take out of the oven, and set aside to cool.

To make the cream filling, in a mixer, beat together the whipping cream, pudding mix, sour cream and granulated sugar until firm and creamy.

Sprinkle half the pecans on the kataifi base in one of the pans and spread the cream filling on them. Sprinkle the remaining pecans over the filling, and crumble the other kataifi base over them, until it covers the top of the cake. Put in the refrigerator for at least 2 hours to set. Serve cold, and keep in the refrigerator.

GRANDMA KNOWS BEST

The classic version of this cake is prepared without the chopped caramelized pecans, but I find that they add a lot of flavor, texture and color. Caramelized pecans can be bought or homemade—see the recipe on page 217.

Nostalgic Chocolate Mousse

The classic—and nostalgic—mousse contains raw eggs—there is no escaping that. The egg yolks give it its shine and velvety texture, and the egg white meringue is responsible for the lightness and fluffiness of the mousse. I am well aware that raw eggs are not everyone's cup of tea, and I am actually on your side, but when it comes to chocolate mousse, all my principles go out the window, and I devour it without giving its contents another thought (I had it like that throughout my childhood and youth, and I came out just fine, thank you). I just hope that the day is not far when pasteurized eggs, like the ones used in confectionery establishments, are available in every grocery store. Until then, make sure you use the freshest eggs, and check for any cracks or dirt on the shell. I do, however, include a chocolate mousse recipe without eggs. It doesn't have the popping air bubbles, but it is creamy and delicious nonetheless, and can be an excellent substitute if you don't want raw eggs in your mousse. Pregnant women and children—you, people, have no choice but to opt for the no-egg recipe.

8 SERVINGS

10½ oz (300g) dark chocolate
½ cup (120ml) water
1 tsp vanilla extract (or rum extract)
1 tbsp (12g) instant coffee powder
6 eggs, separated, at room temperature
½ cup (100g) sugar

Put the chocolate, water, vanilla and coffee in a bowl. Heat in a microwave oven until dissolved, and mix until combined and smooth.

Add the yolks to the chocolate mixture, whisking quickly to prevent curdling.

In a mixer, beat the egg whites for 1 minute at medium speed, until a soft white frost forms. Go on beating and gradually—1 spoonful every 10 seconds—add the sugar. Go on beating for another 2 minutes, until the meringue is shiny and creamy.

Whisk one-third of the meringue into the chocolate mixture. Gently fold in the rest of the meringue, only until combined and airy.

Divide the mousse among personal serving bowls and put in the refrigerator for 2 hours to cool and set. Serve cold.

Chocolate Mousse without Eggs

A little less nostalgic, but still yummy good . . .

6 SERVINGS

2 cups (480ml) whipping cream, divided
7 oz (200g) dark chocolate

In a bowl, combine 1 cup (240ml) of the whipping cream and the chocolate. Heat in a microwave oven until melted, and whisk to combine. Cool to room temperature.

In a mixer, beat the remaining 1 cup (240ml) whipping cream until creamy and soft. Fold the cream into the chocolate mixture.

Divide the mousse among personal serving bowls and put in the refrigerator for 2 hours to cool and set. Serve cold.

Puff Pastry Cones Filled with Whipped Cream

These sweethearts remind me of ice cream cones in the summer. I never use metal cups for them—I much prefer the more available wafer cones used for ice cream. The wafer cones in this recipe are not eaten, but don't throw them away; you can use them again for the same purpose or even enjoy them the way they are meant to be enjoyed—filled with ice cream.

20 SERVINGS

FOR THE PUFF PASTRY CONES
20 pointy wafer ice cream cones

1 lb (500g) frozen, pre-rolled puff pastry, thawed overnight in the refrigerator

1 egg, beaten

About 1 cup (200g) granulated sugar

FOR THE CHOCOLATE COATING
3 oz (100g) dark chocolate

1 tbsp (15 ml) vegetable oil

FOR THE QUICK VANILLA CREAM
1 cup (240ml) whipping cream

1 cup (240ml) milk

½ cup (80g) vanilla-flavored instant pudding mix

Powdered sugar, for garnish (optional)

GRANDMA KNOWS BEST
It is best to fill the cones right before serving them, so that the pastry will not become soggy. The baked—empty—ones keep very well in a sealed container at room temperature for up to a day.

To make the puff pastry cones, preheat the oven to 350°F (180°C). Line a baking sheet with parchment paper. Wrap the cones in aluminum foil (tuck any excess foil into the cone) and thinly grease them.

Lay the puff pastry sheet on your work surface, and cut into 1-inch (2.5-cm) wide strands (it should be a little wider than the final desired result, because during the wrapping process the strands stretch and narrow a little). Wrap the strands around each cone, one at a time, starting from the tip and working your way to the top rims (turn the cone itself and not the pastry strand). When the strand runs out, pinch a new one to it, and continue. Make sure that each rotation overlaps the previous one a little. When finished, the wrapped pastry should reach just shy of the cone's top. Cut the pastry, and tuck the end under the previous lap, to keep it from opening in the oven.

Brush the cones with the egg and roll in the granulated sugar. Lay the cones spaciously on the prepared baking sheet (try to lay the cones with the tip of the pastry strand on the bottom, so it won't open). Bake for 25 minutes, until the cones are nice and brown. Take the cones out of the oven and turn the oven down to 325°F (160°C).

Carefully separate the pastry cones from the wafer ice cream cones and peel off the aluminum foil (careful, it's hot!). The inside is not yet baked, and that's okay. Return the pastry cones to the oven for another 10 minutes, until it is. Let cool completely before coating with chocolate and filling with cream.

To make the chocolate coating, melt the chocolate in a bowl in a microwave oven, then mix in the oil. Dip the top of each pastry cone into the chocolate. Lay on a paper-lined tray and put in the freezer for 1–2 minutes, until the chocolate hardens.

To make the cream, in a mixer, beat together the whipping cream, milk and pudding mix, until creamy and firm. Fill the cones (using a spoon or a piping bag) and serve immediately. You can dust them with powdered sugar for garnish.

Wrap ice cream cones in aluminum foil and grease the foil.

Cut the puff pastry into 1-inch (2.5-cm) wide strands and wrap around each cone.

Bake for 25 minutes. Separate from the wafer cones and return to the oven for another 10 minutes.

The Slip-Slider Cake

Every family has their own code names for foods that only they understand. We dubbed the H-U-G-E, jaw-breaking pastrami sandwich dad used to prepare "Big Mouth," while the orange cut into eight wedges with the peel on was called "Harmonica Orange" and was the only way my sister could be persuaded to eat it. "The Slip-Slider" was mom's most festive cake. It just slipped down the throat and slid straight to the stomach. There is the "Krembo" version, and the one called "Crème on Crème," but the Slip-Slider is like nothing you have ever tasted: a melt-in-your-mouth, no-flour chocolate sponge base (with lots of chocolate!); a cool and velvety layer of vanilla cream (if you peek in the "Grandma Knows Best" section below, you will understand why); and a sweet milk-chocolate and coffee frosting.

ONE 9½-INCH (23.5-CM) CAKE

FOR THE CHOCOLATE SPONGE

7 oz (200g) dark chocolate
½ cup (120ml) whipping cream
6 eggs, at room temperature
½ cup (100g) sugar

FOR THE VANILLA CREAM

2 cups (480ml) whipping cream
¼ cup (50g) sugar
½ cup (80g) vanilla-flavored instant pudding mix
1⅔ cups (400ml) sour cream

FOR THE CHOCOLATE FROSTING

½ cup (120ml) whipping cream
1 tsp instant coffee powder
5 oz (150g) milk chocolate

To make the chocolate sponge, preheat the oven to 350°F (180°C). Line a 9½-inch (23.5-cm) springform pan with a parchment paper circle.

In a bowl, combine the dark chocolate and whipping cream and melt in a microwave oven. Set aside to cool, until the mixture is lukewarm.

In a mixer, beat the eggs and sugar at high speed for 10 minutes, until very thick and fluffy.

Manually fold in the lukewarm chocolate mixture.

Spread the batter in the prepared pan, and bake for 25–30 minutes, until the cake has risen. It will be soft and a little wobbly, and look as if it is not baked all the way through, but it will set during cooling. While the cake is still warm, use a knife to loosen it from the sides of the pan. The cake will drop evenly when chilled, and that's okay.

To make the cream, in a mixer, beat together the whipping cream, sugar, pudding mix and sour cream until creamy and firm. Spread the cream on the cold cake and put in the refrigerator to cool and set (4 hours, or 1 hour in the freezer).

To make the chocolate frosting, put the whipping cream, coffee and milk chocolate in a bowl and melt in a microwave oven. Whisk to combine and cool a little.

Pour the frosting onto the cold cake, and gently shake the pan until the frosting covers the cream. Return to the refrigerator for 10 minutes (or to the freezer for 5) so the frosting can cool and set. Insert a knife between the cake and the sides of the pan to release it. Slice the cake with a knife dipped in boiling water (dip and towel dry between each slice) and serve. Keep in the refrigerator, and serve cold.

GRANDMA KNOWS BEST

Instead of making the usual cream with vanilla-flavored pudding, I upgrade it with sour cream—this brilliant idea belongs to my friend and champion baker from Eilat, Lilach Biton. The sour cream makes it richer while counteracting its heavy sweetness.

Foolproof Cream Puffs

This is a recipe for cream puffs that never ever fails! No more measuring the eggs, one spoon at a time, no more checking and double-checking the thickness of the batter and no more praying when they go into the oven (although praying never hurt anyone). Just follow the instructions to the letter, and they won't "fall" or flatten out and will look gorgeous, fluffy and airy every single time. I guarantee! The milk and butter in the recipe give these cream puffs their melt-in-the-mouth rich flavor; however, the nondairy version—water and margarine instead of milk and butter—works just fine, too.

30 CREAM PUFFS

FOR THE CREAM PUFFS
1 cup (240ml) milk
3½ oz (100g) butter, diced
1 tbsp (12g) granulated sugar
½ tsp salt
1 cup (140g) all-purpose flour
4 eggs

FOR THE FILLING
1 cup (240ml) whipping cream
¾ cup (180ml) milk
½ cup (80g) vanilla-flavored instant pudding mix

FOR SERVING
Powdered sugar or hot chocolate sauce (page 62)

To make the cream puffs, preheat the oven to 350°F (180°C). Line 2 or 3 baking sheets with parchment paper.

In a pot over high heat, combine the milk, butter, granulated sugar and salt and bring to a boil. Take off the stove, add all the flour at once and stir immediately with a wooden spoon for about 1 minute, until a smooth ball of dough is formed and there are no traces of flour.

Transfer the hot dough to the mixer fitted with the flat attachment and beat for 2 minutes at medium speed, until no more steam rises from the dough (which will still be warm).

Crack one egg into a bowl and add to the mixer while beating at medium speed. The dough will turn to smooth flakes for a minute, and come together again. Repeat this step with the rest of the eggs, adding them one at a time (waiting each time for the flaky mixture to bond back into a dough). Every now and then, stop the mixer and scrape the sides of the bowl. After the last egg is added and incorporated, beat for another 1 minute, until the dough is smooth and velvety.

Put the dough into a piping bag with a ½-inch (1.3-cm) wide serrated tip. Pipe 30 little mounds spaciously on the prepared baking sheets. Bake for 20 minutes without opening the oven—the puffs will rise beautifully and turn golden. After 20 minutes, slightly open the oven door to allow the steam to get out and the puffs to dry (you can use a wooden spoon to ensure the door stays slightly ajar) and continue baking like this for another 5 minutes. Take out of the oven, and set aside to cool completely.

To make the filling, in a mixer, beat together the whipping cream, milk and vanilla pudding mix until creamy and firm. Put the filling in a piping bag with a ⅓-inch (8-mm) smooth tip. Insert the piping tip into the base of each puff, and squeeze until it puffs up and the filling starts to peek out. Alternatively (see photo), you can slice each puff horizontally and spoon in the filling. Keep in the refrigerator until you are ready to serve.

Dust with powdered sugar or decorate with a hot chocolate sauce, and serve.

GRANDMA KNOWS BEST

In my family, we like our cream puffs filled with the simplest, instant pudding–based whipped cream; however, if you prefer, you can fill them with a real quality vanilla whipped cream (page 31) or with a coffee-flavored whipped cream (page 17). And I am yet to meet anyone who would say no to a profiterole—sliced cream puffs filled with ice cream and drowned in chocolate sauce.

Swan Cream Puffs

Every time I make these swans, they are the *pièce de résistance* of the dessert table, and people who see them reminisce about their grandmas/moms/aunties/baking magicians who made them. Note: The delicate and slender "head" puffs must be baked separately from the more robust "body" puffs, because the baking times are different.

20 LARGE SWANS

Cream puff dough (page 48)
Vanilla cream (page 21)
Powdered sugar, for serving

GRANDMA KNOWS BEST

Swans need a lake, so here is how to float them on a chocolate one: in a microwave oven, heat ½ cup (120ml) whipping cream with 4 ounces (120g) dark chocolate and 1 tablespoon (20g) honey, and whisk until smooth. Pour the hot sauce onto a serving plate and put the swans on it. Serve immediately.

Preheat the oven to 350°F (180°C). Line 2 baking sheets with parchment paper.

Put three-fourths of the dough into a piping bag with a ½-inch (1.3-cm) wide serrated tip. Put the remaining dough in another piping bag with a ¼-inch (6-mm) thin smooth tip. Pipe the "bodies" and the "heads" onto the prepared baking sheets, as follows: With the wide serrated tip, pipe 20 chubby blobs of dough about 2½ inches (6.4cm) long for the bodies, and with the thin smooth tip, pipe 24 "2" shaped thin strips for the heads (make an extra 4, because some will inevitably break in the assembly process).

Bake the swans' heads for 10 minutes without opening the oven, until golden. Remove, and bake the bodies for 20 minutes without opening the oven. The puffs will rise and turn golden. After 20 minutes, slightly open the oven door to let the steam out and allow the puffs to dry (hold the door in place with a wooden spoon). Continue baking like this for another 5 minutes, then take out of the oven and cool completely.

Put the filling in a piping bag with a ½-inch (1.3-cm) wide serrated tip.

Slice the "body" puffs in half horizontally all the way through (like a bun) and generously pipe cream onto the base. Cut the top half lengthwise and attach each half to the sides of the piped filling, with the cut side facing down. Stick the bottom of the "head" into the filling, dust with powdered sugar, and serve.

Pipe the dough into "heads" and "bodies."

Pipe cream onto the base. Cut the top half lengthwise.

Attach each half and stick the bottom of the "head" into the filling.

HOME-SWEET-HOME CAKES

These cakes are so simple and homey, yet we miss them the most and never leave a crumb of these comforting desserts.

Old-Fashioned Plum Cake

I remember the first time I prepared this cake and brought it my sister's work. Staff and patrons alike devoured it so fast, I couldn't even save one little piece for my sister. "The recipe! Give us the recipe!" they demanded with full mouths. One lady in particular stuck in my memory. She came to me with tears in her eyes, and said that it tasted exactly like her grandma's cake.

That was when I decided to write this book of sweet memories. So, here is the plum cake that had started it all: a melt-in-your-mouth, short-crust pastry base, a layer of sweet plums that turn into a tangy jam in the process of baking and a layer of sweet meringue (to counteract the sourness), all topped with short-crust pastry crumbs mixed with chopped walnuts.

ONE 10-INCH (25-CM) CAKE

FOR THE PLUMS
12 large plums (about 2¼ lb [1 kg])

¼ cup (50g) sugar

1 tsp ground cinnamon

Juice of ½ lemon

FOR THE PASTRY BASE AND CRUMBS
2½ cups (350g) all-purpose flour

1 tsp baking powder

7 oz (200g) butter or margarine, cold and diced

¾ cup (150g) sugar

3 egg yolks (save the whites for the meringue)

Zest of 1 lemon

1 tbsp (15ml) lemon juice

½ cup (50g) chopped walnuts

FOR THE MERINGUE
3 egg whites, at room temperature

¾ cup (150g) sugar

To prepare the plums, cut each plum into 6 wedges and remove the pits. Put the plum wedges in a bowl, add the sugar, cinnamon and lemon juice, and stir to combine. Let the plums soak until it's time to assemble the cake.

To make the pastry base, preheat the oven to 350°F (180°C). Grease a 10-inch (25-cm) springform pan.

Put the flour, baking powder, butter cubes and sugar in a food processor, and mix until crumbs form. Add the egg yolks, lemon zest and juice, and continue mixing in short pulses only until a flaky, slightly dry dough is formed.

Reserve about 1 cup (240g) of this flaky dough, mix with the chopped walnuts and set aside (in summer, keep in the refrigerator). Flatten the remaining dough in the prepared pan. Don't worry about the dough being flaky, just press it tightly and it will be just fine. Strain the plums and place them on the crust.

Bake for 30 minutes, until bubbles form and the plums begin to brown here and there. Take the cake out, but leave the oven on.

To make the meringue, in a mixer, beat the egg whites at medium speed for 1 minute, until a white froth with large bubbles forms. Continue beating while gradually adding the sugar, until the meringue is stiff and shiny.

Spread the meringue over the plums—you should do it quickly and carefully, because the baking pan is hot. Sprinkle the mixture of crumbs and chopped walnuts all over the meringue.

Return the cake to the oven and bake for 25 minutes longer, until the meringue rises very high and the crumbs are golden. Take the cake out (the meringue will sink back to its original volume), and let it cool. Store the cake in the refrigerator.

GRANDMA KNOWS BEST

Don't worry about the pastry being dry and flaky; it'll all smooth out in the oven. If, by mistake, you overmixed and got a smooth, homogenous dough (good for laying down the crust, not so good for making crumbs), no big deal. There are two ways to fix this: add a teaspoon or two of flour to your leftover dough and mix with your hands until it crumbles, or freeze your leftover dough and grate it over the cake.

Apple Cake with Meringue and Crumbs

If grandma had a microwave oven, she would have used it to soften the apples (instead of cooking them in a pot). Combining the apples with jam and pudding gives them the sweetness and thickness they need. The short-crust base, fluffy vanilla-flavored topping and crumbs (which are grated from the leftover dough) create an exciting cake that will take you way back.

ONE 10-INCH (25-CM) CAKE

FOR THE PASTRY BASE AND CRUMBS

2½ cups (350g) all-purpose flour

2 tsp (8g) baking powder

5 tbsp (60g) sugar

7 oz (200g) butter or margarine, cold and diced

5 egg yolks (save the whites for the meringue)

FOR THE FILLING

6 large apples

3 tbsp (45g) apricot jam

¼ cup (40g) vanilla-flavored instant pudding mix

1 tsp ground cinnamon

FOR THE MERINGUE

5 egg whites

1 cup (200g) sugar

¼ cup (40g) vanilla-flavored instant pudding mix

To make the pastry base, preheat the oven to 350°F (180°C). Grease a 10-inch (25-cm) springform pan.

In a food processor, process the flour, baking powder, sugar and butter cubes to a crumb consistency. Add the egg yolks and mix in short pulses, just until a dough is formed.

Wrap one-fourth of the dough in plastic wrap and put in the freezer (to make it easy to grate later). With your hands, flatten the remaining dough on the bottom of the prepared pan and bake for 15 minutes, until it begins to rise and turns golden. Remove from the oven but leave the oven on.

To make the filling, peel, core and thinly slice the apples. Put the apple slices in a microwave-proof bowl, add the apricot jam and mix thoroughly. Cover in plastic wrap, and heat in the microwave oven for 3 minutes at maximum capacity. Take out, mix again and return to the microwave oven for another 3 minutes, until the apples are partially softened and have released a lot of liquid. Take off the plastic wrap (watch out for the hot steam!) and let it cool a little.

Add the pudding mix and cinnamon to the apples and stir to combine (the pudding mix will turn the liquid into a sauce). Set aside.

To make the meringue, in a mixer, beat the egg whites at medium speed for 1 minute, until a white froth with large air bubbles forms. Go on beating and gradually add the sugar until meringue is shiny and firm. Lower mixer's speed to minimum, add the pudding mix and go on beating slowly for another few seconds, only until combined.

Spread the lukewarm apple filling on the baked pastry base. Spread the meringue over the apples. Take the remaining dough out of the freezer, and grate it over the meringue, using the large holes of the grater, until covered.

Return it to the oven and bake for 35 minutes, until the meringue rises very high and the crumbs turn golden. Take out of the oven (the meringue will return to its original volume). Let the cake cool before taking it out of the pan and serving. Store in the refrigerator.

Tall Orange Lekach

Whether you call it lekach, tort, chiffon, sponge, coffee cake or *jeunesse*, this one is by far the most homey and comforting cake to have with your coffee. Our grandmothers would whip it up without effort or fuss. If we want the same tall (very tall) result that doesn't fall, we must stick to the instructions. For those of us who don't mind any torte, there is a "lazy" version on page 70.

ONE 10-INCH (25-CM) CAKE

7 eggs, separated, at room temperature

2 cups (400g) sugar, divided

1 cup (240ml) vegetable oil

Zest of 1 orange

1½ cups (360ml) orange juice

2½ cups (350g) all-purpose flour

2 tsp (8g) baking powder

Preheat the oven to 325°F (160°C). Have ready a 10-inch (25-cm) Bundt pan (do not grease).

In a mixer, at high speed, beat the egg yolks with 1 cup (200 g) of the sugar for 5 minutes, until light and fluffy (the sugar will not dissolve, but that's okay). Lower the mixer's speed and add the oil in a slow drizzle. Add the orange zest and juice, and beat to combine. Add the flour and baking powder and beat at low speed for another minute, until all lumps are smoothed out. Transfer to a large bowl and set aside.

Thoroughly clean the mixer bowl and the whisk attachment (for the egg whites). In the clean mixer bowl, beat the egg whites at low to medium speed (if your mixer has a numeric scale of 1–10, on 4–5 at the most) until soft white froth forms. This should take about 2 minutes. While beating, add the remaining 1 cup (200g) sugar, 1 tablespoon (12g) at a time, at 10-second intervals. After all the sugar is added, turn up the speed to maximum, and beat for another 3 minutes, until airy, shiny and firm (but still creamy).

Add one-third of the meringue to the egg yolk mixture, and whisk until combined. Gently fold in the remaining meringue until combined.

Spread the batter in the ungreased pan (this is very important to ensure that the cake doesn't fall when cooled). Put the cake pan on a baking sheet (not on the rack directly), and put it in the lower third of the hot oven. Bake for 1 hour and 10 minutes, until the cake has risen and is firm to the touch and a skewer inserted in its center comes out completely dry (a toothpick will be too short, because this is a very tall cake). If the cake is not baked all the way through, it will fall when cooled. Take out of the oven and cool. The cake will deflate a little, but that's okay—it should resume its pre-baking volume.

Pass a knife all around between the cake and the pan's sides to release it, and turn it over onto a serving platter. Keep covered at room temperature.

GRANDMA KNOWS BEST

The beating instructions in this recipe are especially detailed, because this cake will literally rise and fall on the correct beating. Follow these instructions, taking special care to begin beating the egg whites at medium (not high!) speed, ensuring a firm but creamy meringue.

AND ANOTHER THING

The grandmothers used to turn the baked cake in the pan upside down over a glass bottle, so that reverse gravity would prevent its falling. In this case, it is not necessary; just follow the instructions to the letter, and the cake will come out tall and firm (knock on wood). If you insist, get the special Bundt pan with three little "legs" protruding from the top; they serve the same purpose.

Chocolate-Coated Poppy Seed Lekach

Even though this grandma cake is coated with chocolate, it is still in the have-with-your-tea-or-coffee "simple cake" category. It is so airy that I don't consider it sinful or decadent (which is just as well, because I can't stop eating it). Soaking the poppy seeds in water is important, because it makes the cake moist—don't skip it (see the "Grandma Knows Best" section below).

ONE 10-INCH (25-CM) CAKE

FOR THE POPPY SEEDS
1 cup (100g) poppy seeds
1½ cups (360ml) boiling water

FOR THE CAKE
7 eggs, separated, at room temperature
½ cup (120ml) vegetable oil
1 tsp vanilla extract
Zest of 1 lemon
2½ cups (350g) all-purpose flour
2 tsp (8g) baking powder
1½ cups (300g) sugar

FOR THE CHOCOLATE FROSTING
½ cup (120ml) whipping cream
4 oz (120g) dark chocolate

GRANDMA KNOWS BEST
Poppy seed cakes may be too dense and dry, because the poppy seeds "drink up" the liquids during baking. This particular recipe is soft and moist due to a sweet little secret: The poppy seeds are pre-soaked in water, absorb some of it and soften. Soaking the poppy seeds has another bonus—it takes away any natural bitterness. The boiling water may be substituted with hot milk.

To prepare the poppy seeds, in a bowl, combine the poppy seeds and boiling water. Set aside for 10 minutes, until slightly cooled (the poppy seeds will not absorb all the water, and that's okay).

To make the cake, preheat the oven to 350°F (180°C). Have ready a 10-inch (25-cm) Bundt pan (do not grease).

In the largest bowl you have in your house, whisk together the egg yolks, oil, vanilla, lemon zest and the soaked poppy seeds (soaking water included). Add the flour and baking powder, and whisk for another 1 minute, until all lumps are smoothed out.

In a mixer, beat the egg whites at low to medium speed (if your mixer has a numeric scale of 1–10, on 4–5 at the most) until soft white froth forms. This takes about 2 minutes. While beating, add the sugar 1 tablespoon (12g) at a time, at 10-second intervals. After all the sugar is added, turn up the speed to maximum, and beat for another 3 minutes, until airy, shiny and firm (but still creamy).

Add one-third of the meringue to the egg yolk mixture, and whisk until combined. Gently fold in the remaining meringue, until combined.

Spread the batter in the ungreased pan (this is very important to ensure that the cake doesn't fall when cooled). Put the cake pan on a baking sheet (not on the rack directly), and put it in the lower one-third of the hot oven. Bake for 1 hour, until the cake has risen and is firm to the touch and a skewer inserted in its center comes out completely dry (a toothpick will be too short, because this is a very tall cake). If the cake is not baked all the way through, it will fall when cooled. Take out of the oven and let cool. The cake will deflate a little, but that's okay—it should resume its pre-baking volume.

To make the chocolate frosting, in a small pot, bring the whipping cream almost to a boil, remove from the stove, add the chocolate and mix until dissolved.

Pass a knife around the edges of the cake to release it. Turn it out onto a serving plate. Pour the chocolate frosting on the cake and put in the freezer for 5 minutes, so the frosting will set. To serve, slice the cake with a knife dipped in boiling water.

Fluffy Chocolate Marble Lekach

I love showing off this tall, airy cake that melts in your mouth like a soft cloud. Don't let its humble reputation confuse you; its texture is to die for, and its rich flavor is reminiscent of a scrumptious chocolate yeast roulade. The secret here is a hot chocolate sauce (without a drop of chocolate) poured into the lekach batter. This creates moist and sweet "chocolate" swirls in the airy cake, and the smell that fills the house when this cake is baking is simply indescribable.

ONE 10-INCH (25-CM) CAKE

FOR THE CHOCOLATE SAUCE
¼ cup (60ml) water
⅓ cup (70g) sugar
¼ cup (40g) cocoa
3½ tbsp (50g) butter

FOR THE CAKE
7 eggs, separated, at room temperature
1 tsp vanilla extract
½ cup (120ml) vegetable oil
1 cup (240ml) water
Zest of ½ orange
2½ cups (350g) all-purpose flour
2 tsp (8g) baking powder
1¼ cups (250g) sugar

GRANDMA KNOWS BEST

How in the world can we release the cake if the pan is not greased?! Well, the cake must be cooled, or it will break into pieces. When it is cold, pass a knife between the cake and the sides of the pan. Put the serving platter over the pan and turn. Hold the pan firmly on the plate—and then give it one good up-and-down shake—the cake will separate and "land" neatly on the plate.

To make the chocolate sauce, in a small pot, combine the water, sugar, cocoa and butter and heat, stirring, until a smooth sauce forms. Remove from the stove, and let cool a little.

To make the cake, preheat the oven to 350°F (180°C). Have ready a 10-inch (25-cm) Bundt pan (do not grease).

In the largest bowl you have in your house, whisk together the egg yolks, vanilla, oil, water and orange zest. Add the flour and baking powder, and whisk vigorously for about 1 minute, until combined (the batter will be very thick, and that's okay).

In a mixer, beat the egg whites at low to medium speed (if your mixer has a numeric scale of 1–10, on 4–5 at the most) until a soft white froth forms. This takes about 2 minutes. While beating, add the sugar 1 tablespoon (12g) at a time, at 10-second intervals. After all the sugar is added, turn up the speed to maximum, and beat for another 3 minutes, until airy, shiny and firm (but still creamy).

Add one-third of the meringue to the egg yolk mixture, and whisk until combined. Gently fold in the remaining meringue until combined.

Pour the chocolate sauce into the batter and, with a spoon, swirl two or three times (not more!) in a downward motion. It doesn't look pretty just yet, but have no fear—when you pour it into the pan, the marble effect will happen.

Pour the batter into the ungreased Bundt pan (very important, or the cake will fall when cooled!). Shake the pan a little to level the batter. Put the cake pan on a baking sheet (not directly on the rack), and put it in the lower one-third of the hot oven. Bake for about 1 hour, until the cake is golden and spongy to the touch and a skewer inserted in its center comes out with a little chocolate but with no crumbs. The cake must be baked all the way through, or it will fall when cooled. Take out of the oven and set aside to cool. The cake will deflate a little, but that's okay—it should resume its pre-baking volume.

Pass a knife around the cake to release it, and flip over onto a serving plate. Keep covered at room temperature.

Insanely Soft Marble Cake

The name says it all: a soft marble cake. Insanely so. The softness is achieved by the whipped eggs (don't worry—whole eggs, no need to separate); the moistness comes from the oil and the orange juice; the fragrance from the vanilla; and the flavor comes from the melted chocolate mixed into the batter. Yes, your mixer is going to get dirty, but believe me, the grandmothers had it worse; they had to do all of it by hand . . .

3 LOAF CAKES OR 2 HEART-SHAPED CAKES

FOR THE BATTER
4 eggs, at room temperature

1½ cups (300g) sugar

1 tsp vanilla extract

1 cup (240ml) vegetable oil

1 cup (240ml) orange juice

½ cup (120ml) water

2½ cups (350g) all-purpose flour

1 tbsp (10g) baking powder

FOR THE CHOCOLATE MIXTURE
3½ oz (100g) dark chocolate, melted

1 tbsp (15ml) vegetable oil

To make the batter, preheat the oven to 350°F (180°C). Grease 3 loaf pans or 2 heart-shaped pans.

In a mixer, at high speed, beat together the eggs, sugar and vanilla for 10 minutes, until the mixture is light in color and thick, resembling a mousse consistency. Lower the mixer to the minimum speed and slowly drizzle in the oil while beating. Add the orange juice and water in the same way. Add the flour and baking powder, and beat slowly, until the batter is smooth. Put three-fourths of the batter into the pans.

To make the chocolate mixture, combine the melted chocolate and oil. Add the chocolate mixture to the remaining quarter of the batter and mix until combined. Spoon the chocolate batter over the white batter in the pans. Insert a knife in the batter, all the way through, and swirl to create the marble effect. Repeat in the other pan(s).

Bake for 40–45 minutes, until the cakes are springy and a toothpick inserted in their centers comes out almost dry. Let cool before serving.

GRANDMA KNOWS BEST
Find another marble sponge—of the dense and buttery kind (in a good way)—on page 62.

...this coffee cake came out of the oven, I immediately knew what it should be called. I am well aware of the fact that there is a cake dubbed "Perfect" in *Sweet Secrets*, but now there is another contender. Any other name would not do it justice. The list of ingredients looks suspiciously short, but it will produce a cake that will blow your mind—and all your senses—away. And I have not yet told you how easy it is to make; you make the crumble in a food processor, take a cup of it out and add the rest of the ingredients and that's that—you have a cake batter. The velvety cake is covered with crispy crumbs, and all that glory simply melts in your mouth!

2 LOAF CAKES

7 oz (200g) butter, softened

1 cup (200g) sugar

2½ cups (350g) all-purpose flour

3 eggs

¾ cup (200ml) sour cream

1 tbsp (10g) baking powder

1 tsp vanilla extract

Preheat the oven to 350°F (180°C). Grease 2 loaf pans.

In a food processor, combine the butter, sugar and flour only until you get a flaky consistency. Take out 1 cup (240g) of the crumbs and reserve (make sure you do this part with the food processor turned off, and only with a spoon!).

Add the eggs, sour cream, baking powder and vanilla to the remaining mixture in the food processor, and mix for another 15–20 seconds, just until combined and smooth.

Spread the batter in the prepared pans and sprinkle the crumbs on top. If the crumbs mixture is a little lumpy, break it by hand. The batter should fill only half of the pans—these cakes rise a lot in the oven.

Bake for about 40 minutes, until the cakes have risen and are spongy to the touch, the crumbs are golden and a toothpick inserted into the center comes out almost dry. Let cool before slicing.

GRANDMA KNOWS BEST

You can use this recipe for muffins—scoop the batter (an ice cream scoop is the best for it) into the cavities in a muffin tray, sprinkle 1 tablespoon (15g) of crumbs on each one, and bake for 20 minutes at 375°F (190°C). This recipe makes 20 muffins.

Grandma's Semolina-Coconut Cake

I had forgotten this cake over the years (when I was little, it was a standard cake in almost every household, and I had it many times), and then, one day, I tasted it in a well-known Israeli coffee chain, and I was immediately overwhelmed by nostalgia. A few phone calls and experiments in the kitchen later, I succeeded in re-creating the familiar flavor. This semolina cake gets its moistness from a syrup poured on it after baking. I have since made it so many times that it is one of the very few recipes I remember by heart.

ONE 13 X 11-INCH (33 X 28-CM) CAKE

FOR THE CAKE
4 eggs, separated
¾ cup (180ml) vegetable oil
1 cup (240ml) orange juice
1 cup (160g) semolina
1 cup (140g) all-purpose flour
1 tbsp (10g) baking powder
1 cup (100g) desiccated coconut
¾ cup (150g) sugar

FOR THE SYRUP
1 cup (240ml) water
1 cup (200g) sugar
2 tbsp (30ml) lemon juice

FOR GARNISH
½ cup (50g) desiccated coconut

To make the cake, preheat the oven to 350°F (180°C). Grease a 13 x 11-inch (33 x 28-cm) baking pan.

In a bowl, whisk together the egg yolks, oil and orange juice.

In a separate large bowl, mix together the semolina, flour, baking powder and desiccated coconut. Pour the yolk mixture into the semolina mixture, and whisk until incorporated.

In a mixer, beat the egg whites at medium speed for about 1 minute, until they turn to a soft white froth with large bubbles. While beating, gradually add the sugar, and beat until the meringue is firm and shiny.

Add the meringue to the semolina mixture and fold in with a spatula, until combined. Spread the batter in the prepared pan and bake for 30–35 minutes, until the cake is golden and a toothpick inserted in its center comes out dry.

A little before the cake comes out of the oven, prepare the syrup. In a pot, bring the water and sugar to a boil. Cook for 2 minutes, and remove from the stove.

Add the lemon juice to the syrup and stir to combine.

Using a spoon, carefully pour the hot syrup over the hot cake—one spoonful at a time—until all the syrup is "drunk" by the cake.

Sprinkle the desiccated coconut on top, and set aside to cool completely. Keep at room temperature.

GRANDMA KNOWS BEST

If fresh oranges are available, squeeze your own fruit juice. If not, store-bought orange juice or juice prepared with frozen orange concentrate will do the job just fine.

A Winner Orange Coffee Cake

When I am not in the mood for intricate projects, i.e., separating eggs, I substitute the Tall Orange Lekach (page 58) with this super airy, never-fail coffee cake, which takes just few minutes to make—you just whisk everything together and off it goes into the oven.

ONE 10-INCH (25-CM) CAKE

FOR THE CAKE

1½ cups (300g) granulated sugar, plus more for sprinkling

4 eggs

1 cup (240ml) vegetable oil

Zest of 2 oranges

1 cup (240ml) orange juice

2½ cups (350g) all-purpose flour

1 tbsp (10g) baking powder

FOR FINISHING THE CAKE

½ cup (120ml) orange juice

Powdered sugar (about 2 tbsp [20g])

To make the cake, preheat the oven to 325°F (160°C). Grease a 10-inch (25-cm) Bundt pan. Sprinkle with a little granulated sugar to prevent sticking.

In a bowl, whisk together the eggs, granulated sugar, oil, orange zest and orange juice until incorporated. Add the flour and baking powder, and whisk again until combined.

Pour the batter into the prepared pan, and bake for 40 minutes, until the cake is golden and a toothpick inserted in its center comes out almost dry.

To finish the cake, if you want the cake to be moist, spoon the orange juice evenly over it. Cool and dust with powdered sugar for garnish.

GRANDMA KNOWS BEST

I like to wet the cake with orange juice when it is still warm, to make absolutely sure it will be moist. If you prefer it dry, skip this stage—it will still be fabulous.

English Coffee Cake with Candied Citrus Peels

This cake is based on a classic coffee cake, to which I add candied citrus peels. You can make these at home (see page 214), but I like the store-bought colorful ones, because they give the cake its signature taste and a nostalgic look. Now, with your permission, a personal message to my sister, Dana: Before you ask, sis, the answer is, Yes—this is Mom's marble cake recipe from our childhood, which I am forced to dictate to you again and again, because you keep losing it (in "Grandma Knows Best" below, you'll find a little twist in the "plot"). Well, now it is in a book, so there.

2 LOAF CAKES

7 oz (200g) butter, softened

1½ cups (300g) sugar

1 tsp vanilla extract

3 eggs

2½ cups (350g) all-purpose flour

1 tbsp (10g) baking powder

¾ cup (200ml) sour cream

1 cup (225g) candied citrus peels, chopped

Preheat the oven to 350°F (180°C). Grease 2 loaf pans.

In a mixer fitted with the flat attachment, mix the butter, sugar and vanilla at medium speed for 2 minutes, to a creamy consistency. Add the eggs, one at a time (add the next one only after the previous one is incorporated), and mix until combined.

In a separate bowl, combine the flour and baking powder. Lower the mixer's speed and alternately add the flour mixture and the sour cream (in 2 or 3 additions—start and finish with the flour). Add the citrus peels, and mix only until they are evenly distributed in the batter.

Spread the batter in the prepared pans, and bake for 40–45 minutes, until the cakes have browned, are springy to the touch, and a toothpick inserted in their center comes out almost dry (with moist crumbs). Cool and serve. Keep covered at room temperature.

GRANDMA KNOWS BEST

You can use this recipe to make a great marble cake—albeit not so light and fluffy as the Insanely Soft Marble Cake on page 65. Instead of adding the citrus peels, mix half of the batter with 2 heaping tablespoons (20g) of cocoa powder (or chocolate milk mix) melted in 2 tablespoons (30ml) of boiling water. Spread the dark and white batters on top of each other or in alternating layers in the two pans, swirl a little to get a marble effect, and bake the same way.

Layered Apple Coffee Cake of Your Dreams

What makes this cake so dreamy are the two layers of apples soaked in sugar and cinnamon, which are spread between two layers of batter, so the apples in the cake become soft, while those on top brown and crisp up. To do this cake justice, I like to bake it in an old-time aluminum Bundt pan as a gift (the Bundt pan is included).

ONE 10-INCH (25-CM) CAKE

FOR THE APPLE MIXTURE

6 large apples

¼ cup (50g) sugar

1 heaping tsp ground cinnamon

FOR THE CAKE

3 cups (420g) all-purpose flour

1 tbsp (10g) baking powder

1 tsp baking soda

½ tsp salt

1 cup (240ml) vegetable oil

4 eggs

2 cups (400g) sugar

1 tsp vanilla extract

½ cup (120ml) water

To make the apple mixture, peel, core and dice the apples. Place in a bowl, add the sugar and cinnamon, and mix well. Set aside until you are ready to assemble the cake.

To make the cake, preheat the oven to 325°F (160°C). Grease a 10-inch (25-cm) Bundt pan.

Into a large bowl, sift the flour, baking powder, baking soda and salt.

In a separate bowl, whisk together the oil, eggs, sugar, vanilla and water. Pour the wet mixture into the flour mixture, and mix only until a thick and smooth batter forms.

Strain the diced apples. You are welcome to drink the small amount of juice from the straining, because it is not used in this recipe. Pour half of the batter into the prepared pan, and spread half of the apples on top. Repeat with the other half of batter and remaining apples.

Bake for 1 hour and 20 minutes (fear not—the long baking will not diminish the cake's moistness), until a toothpick inserted in its center comes out dry. Cool before slicing. Keep covered at room temperature.

GRANDMA KNOWS BEST

This recipe is so old, the amount of liquids in it were measured in empty eggshells ("Fill an eggshell 8 times with water"). Makes you appreciate today's measuring cups!

Apple and Crumb Cake

This seemingly straightforward recipe demands the most intricate development process, because the taste and texture must be just so. This innocent apple cake was a lot of work. It took dozens of trials and errors until I was satisfied that the crust was crispy enough, the crumbs on top melted in the mouth, the apples in the middle were light, sweet and caramelized to perfection, and the cake maintained its shape and was easy to slice, even when hot. With this winning recipe, preparation is—well—a piece of cake, and if you adhere to the instructions, your cake will also be perfect. This cake is magnificent any way you serve it, and there are several options: cold, hot, spooned straight from the pan or dusted with powdered sugar with a scoop of ice cream on top, and it is superb.

ONE 9½-INCH (24-CM) CAKE

FOR THE CRUST AND CRUMBS
3 cups (420g) all-purpose flour
½ cup (100g) granulated sugar
1 tsp vanilla extract
9 oz (250g) butter, softened

FOR THE APPLE FILLING
10 large Granny Smith apples
3½ oz (50g) butter
½ cup (100g) granulated sugar
½ cup (120g) brown sugar
1 heaping tbsp (10g) cornstarch
2 tbsp (30ml) water

To make the crust and crumbs, preheat the oven to 350°F (180°C). Grease a 9½-inch (24-cm) pie pan.

In a food processor, process the flour, granulated sugar, vanilla and butter until fine, dry crumbs form. Press half of the crumb mixture into the pan to form the crust. Keep the remaining crumbs for later (in the summer, put it in the refrigerator). Bake for about 20 minutes, until golden (in the meantime, prepare the apples). Take out of the oven, but keep it on.

To make the apple filling, peel the apples, remove the cores and cut each apple into 8 wedges.

In a wide pot, melt the butter. Add the apples and the two kinds of sugar, and cook over high heat for 5 minutes, stirring, until the sugars have dissolved, to get a brown, relatively runny sauce. Lower the heat, cover the pot, and cook for another 10 minutes, stirring occasionally, until the apples have softened and the pot is full of liquid.

Dissolve the cornstarch in the water. Add to the pot, turn up the heat and boil for 30 seconds, only until the liquid has turned into a thick sauce and coats the apples.

Spread the hot apples over the baked crust, and spread the reserved crumbs over the apple layer.

Bake for about 30 minutes, until the crumb layer is golden. Cool a little before slicing and serving. Keep in the refrigerator.

GRANDMA KNOWS BEST

The crust comes out hard and crispy, and I think it is lovely like that. If you prefer it softer, add to half of the crumbs that are used for the crust 2 tablespoons (30ml) water or an egg yolk, and knead it a little, until the crumbs become a dough, which is then pressed down in the pan and baked exactly as described above.

Grandma Nicky's Cheese and Raisin Cake

When I have a bad day and need some positivity, there are some comforts that never fail me, like a tacky chick flick accompanied by the largest popcorn bucket, or a lengthy talk on the phone with my mom about nothing and everything ("Seriously? I have gone out and come back, and you are still on the phone?!"). Very high on this list of comforts is a chubby slice of this particular cake, with the short-crust pastry encasing the deliciously guilty pleasure of cheese and raisins in a soft hug. This recipe was given to me by my mom, Nicole, who is also Grandma Nicky to Adam and Emma.

ONE 13 X 11-INCH (33 X 28-CM) CAKE

FOR THE DOUGH
3½ cups (500g) all-purpose flour

2 tsp (8g) baking powder

1 cup (200g) granulated sugar

7 oz (200g) butter, cold and diced

2 eggs

FOR THE CHEESE AND RAISIN FILLING
1 lb (450g) cream cheese

1 lb (450g) Greek yogurt

¾ cup (200ml) sour cream

½ cup (80g) vanilla-flavored pudding mix

2 eggs

1 cup (200g) granulated sugar

Zest of 1 lemon

1 cup (150g) golden raisins

Powdered sugar, for serving

To make the dough, preheat the oven to 350°F (180°C). Grease a 13 x 11-inch (33 x 28-cm) baking pan.

In a food processor, process the flour, baking powder, granulated sugar and butter cubes to a crumbly consistency. Add the eggs and mix again, just until a dough is formed. Press two-thirds of the dough into the prepared pan to form the base. Wrap the remaining dough in plastic wrap, and put in the freezer to partially set, at least 20 minutes. Bake for 20 minutes, until golden, then remove from the oven but leave the oven on.

To make the cheese filling, in a bowl, whisk together the cream cheese, yogurt, sour cream, pudding mix, eggs, granulated sugar and lemon zest to a homogenous mixture. Fold in the raisins.

Spread the cheese filling over the hot cake base. Take the remaining dough out of the freezer and grate it through the large holes of a grater over the cheese filling. Return the cake to the oven and bake for another 40 minutes, until golden and firm.

Set aside to cool, and put in the refrigerator for about 4 hours before serving. Dust with powdered sugar.

GRANDMA KNOWS BEST
The lemon zest gives this cake its old-timey flavor; however, it is optional.

Hotel Cheesecake

Assorted cheeses, an endless salad bar, different quiches, cereals of every variety under the sun, various (and many) fresh breads and . . . wait a minute, over there they make the fried eggs of your choice—help! How can anyone eat all of that and still have room for dessert? So, after the second trip to the breakfast buffet, I breathe, undo one button and brace myself for what's coming next—what I look forward to the most—the hotel's hot, soft, melt-in-your-mouth cheesecake, dusted with powdered sugar (to which I add the maple syrup I secretly took off the pancake tray). Well, here is the homemade version of a cake that tastes like a vacation.

ONE 13 X 11-INCH (33 X 28-CM) CAKE

3 cups (750g) cream cheese

3 cups (750g) Greek yogurt

1¼ cups (250g) granulated sugar

6 eggs

½ cup (80g) vanilla-flavored instant pudding mix

¼ cup (40g) all-purpose flour

¼ cup (40g) cornstarch

1 cup (150g) raisins (optional)

Maple syrup or honey, for serving

Preheat the oven to 300°F (150°C). Put a deep pan with boiling water on the oven's floor (to create a steamy environment). Grease a 13 x 11-inch (33 x 28-cm) baking pan.

In a large bowl, whisk together the cream cheese, yogurt and granulated sugar, and set aside for 5 minutes, until the sugar is dissolved. Whisk in (don't beat!) the eggs.

Pour about one-third of the batter into a smaller bowl, to which you add the pudding mix, flour and cornstarch. Whisk well, until all lumps are smoothed out. Return the cheese and flour mixture to the large bowl and stir to combine. Fold in the raisins (if you want).

Pour the cheese mixture into the prepared pan, and bake for about 1 hour and 15 minutes, until the edges have risen and the cake is almost completely firm (slightly wobbly when the pan is shaken). The cake should stay light in color (with just a hint of gold).

Let cool a little, until the cake resumes its original volume and is set enough for slicing, 10–30 minutes, depending on how (im)patient you are.

Cut into small squares, drizzle with maple syrup and serve in the pan (that's how they do it in the hotel). Keep in the refrigerator, and warm before serving again (instructions below).

GRANDMA KNOWS BEST

This cake is not, nor should it be, "airy." When served warm, it is very soft, but after it has spent some time in the refrigerator, it is much less tasty. There is a simple solution for this problem: Always heat the cake before serving it. You can heat individual slices in the microwave oven, or the entire cake in an oven, preheated to 350°F (180°C), with a bath of boiling water on its floor to prevent drying.

Old-Fashioned Birthday Cake

Once upon a time, long before the "Triple Chocolate Mousse Cakes," there was a simple birthday cake called . . . "Birth-day-cake." To me, this humble cake represents the birthday parties of yesteryear, with a wreath of wildflowers on the birthday girl or boy's head, playing "Pin the Tail on the Donkey" and "Pass the Parcel" or rummaging for sweets in a bowl of flour. Everything was simpler then, in a good way. The plate in the picture here—just like me—dates back to 1974. In honor of my arrival, my parents ordered a set of china with my name on it (the cup broke). As a little girl, I was never allowed to eat from it, for fear it would break. Maybe now, having immortalized it on film, I will take it out of the display cabinet . . .

ONE 10-INCH (25-CM) CAKE

7 oz (200g) margarine or butter

3½ oz (100g) dark chocolate

1 tsp cornstarch

½ cup (120ml) water

3 tbsp (30g) cocoa powder

1½ cups (300g) sugar, divided

1 tsp vanilla or rum extract (or a cap of cognac)

7 eggs, separated, at room temperature

8 heaping tbsp (120g) all-purpose flour

1 tbsp (10g) baking powder

GRANDMA KNOWS BEST

The only thing that bothers me in this otherwise great nostalgic recipe is the fact that the egg yolks are raw, so, to make sure there is no salmonella in this cake, the mixture is pasteurized by heating it until it reaches 162°F (72°C) or by letting it simmer for 3 minutes at 140°F (60°C). To prevent the yolks from cooking and becoming scrambled eggs, I add the cornstarch (just like with crème pâtissière). Apart from this minor change, this recipe is true to the original.

In a small pot over medium-low heat, melt together the margarine and chocolate until dissolved.

In a small bowl, stir the cornstarch into the water until dissolved, and add to the pot with the chocolate mixture. Add the cocoa powder, 1 cup (200g) of the sugar, vanilla and egg yolks. Continue cooking over low heat, constantly stirring, until steam begins to rise and small bubbles form around the edges. The mixture must reach the stage of near boiling only, to pasteurize the yolks (if you have a thermometer, it should be 162°F [72°C]). Remove from the stove.

Transfer the mixture to a large bowl, and set aside to cool, until the mixture is lukewarm.

Preheat the oven to 350°F (180°C). Grease a 10-inch (25-cm) springform pan.

Take out about a quarter of the mixture (1 cup [130 g]), and keep in the refrigerator to use as frosting.

Add the flour and baking powder to the remaining mixture in the large bowl and whisk until incorporated and smooth.

In a mixer, beat the egg whites at medium speed, until they turn into a white soft froth. Gradually add the remaining ½ cup (100g) sugar, and beat until the meringue is very shiny, airy and firm (but still creamy).

Whisk a third of the meringue into the chocolate batter. Gently fold in the remaining meringue, until the batter is homogenous and fluffy.

Spread the batter in the prepared pan and bake for about 50 minutes, until the cake is spongy to the touch and a toothpick inserted in its center comes out with moist crumbs. Let cool.

Spread the reserved mixture over the cake. Keep in the refrigerator, and serve cold or at room temperature . . . and—happy birthday!

A Gigantic Black (Chocolate) Cake for 40 Kids

Yes, it is a simple cake, but it is so soft and chocolaty that people are always pestering me about the recipe. This enormous version is for large-scale birthday parties. The cake comes out tall, and cut into squares, it easily feeds 40 hungry participants (actually, it divides into 42 squares, but—hey—isn't the baker entitled to a couple?). The quantities in this recipe are not for the faint-hearted, but remember—this cake weighs more than 6½ pounds (3kg). If you prefer a more standard scale, see the instructions In "Grandma Knows Best" below.

ONE 15½ X 12-INCH (40 X 30.5-CM) CAKE

FOR THE CAKE
4 eggs

2 cups (480ml) vegetable oil

4¼ cups (1L) lukewarm water

4 cups (560g) all-purpose flour

2 heaping tbsp (20g) baking powder

4 cups (800g) sugar

1 cup (140g) cocoa powder

1 cup (140g) chocolate-milk mix

FOR THE FROSTING
1 cup (240ml) whipping cream

7 oz (200g) dark chocolate

Colored sprinkles, for decorating

To make the cake, preheat the oven to 325°F (160°C). Grease a deep oven tray or an aluminum (disposable) extra-large 15½ x 12-inch (40 x 30.5-cm) pan.

In the biggest bowl you can get your hands on, whisk together the eggs, oil and water.

In a separate large bowl, combine the flour, baking powder, sugar, cocoa powder and chocolate-milk mix.

Gradually, 1 cup (140g) at a time, add the dry ingredients to the egg mixture, whisking well after each addition. After all the dry ingredients have been added, whisk for another minute, until the batter is homogenous, creamy and lump-free.

Pour the batter into the prepared pan and bake for 40 minutes, until the cake is springy and a toothpick inserted in its center comes out almost dry (with moist crumbs). Let cool a little.

To make the frosting, in a microwave oven, heat the whipping cream and chocolate and whisk into a smooth sauce. Pour over the cake, and tilt it in a circular motion for full coverage. Put in the freezer for 5 minutes to set, and only then decorate with the colored sprinkles. If the chocolate frosting is not cold and set, the sprinkles will sink into it. Keep in the refrigerator.

Slice the cake with a knife dipped in boiling water like so: 5 lengthwise cuts and 6 widthwise cuts, to get 7 rows and 6 columns (42 squares). Serve cold or at room temperature.

GRANDMA KNOWS BEST
Freaked out by the quantities? No problem—you can make a "normal" round cake by simply measuring half of everything in this recipe, pouring the batter into a 9½-inch (24-cm) springform pan, and baking for 50 minutes at 325°F (160°C). Prepare half the amount of frosting, then frost and serve.

GRANDMA'S SPECIAL

In olden-day confectionary shops, these treats were the star
of the display window. Nowadays, with a precise recipe, a mixer
and a pinch of patience, everyone can do it.

Checkerboard Cake

The eyes "eat" this cake first; look how gorgeous it is! You admire it from the outside, and then you take a bite . . . and the rich chocolate-vanilla flavor of the cake and creaminess of the vanilla frosting take you way back.

This should have been a tricky and messy project, and the result can be asymmetrical and altogether disappointing, but I am pretty sure I discovered a foolproof way to do it without the piping bags and special pans! The miracle occurred one day, when I was baking Target Cookies (page 134), and realized that the idea could be translated into the Checkerboard Cake. You need two cakes—one vanilla and one chocolate—and they must be identical in size. It is very easy to construct the checkerboard pattern with these two cakes, as is shown in the next couple of pages.

ONE 9-INCH (23-CM) FOUR-LAYER CAKE

FOR THE CAKES
7 eggs, at room temperature
2 cups (400g) sugar
1 tsp vanilla extract
1 cup (240ml) vegetable oil
1 cup (240ml) orange juice
3 cups (420g) all-purpose flour
1 tbsp (10g) baking powder

FOR ADDING TO THE CHOCOLATE CAKE
1 heaping tbsp (15g) cocoa powder
1 heaping tbsp (15g) chocolate-milk mix
2 tbsp (30ml) boiling water

FOR THE CHOCOLATE FILLING (THE "GLUE" BETWEEN THE LAYERS)
1 cup (250g) chocolate spread
½ cup (120ml) boiling water

FOR THE FROSTING
1 cup (240ml) whipping cream
1 cup (240ml) milk
½ cup (80g) vanilla-flavored instant pudding mix

GRANDMA KNOWS BEST

For symmetry's sake, it is very important to measure the circles exactly before you cut them. If they are not precise, you will not get the sharp result you want, and the cake's beauty will be compromised.

To make the cakes, preheat the oven to 325°F (160°C). Line 2 identical 9-inch (23-cm) round cake pans with circles of parchment paper, and grease the paper.

In a mixer, beat the eggs, sugar and vanilla for 10 minutes at high speed, until the mixture is light and fluffy like mousse. Lower the mixer's speed to minimum, and slowly drizzle in the oil followed by the orange juice. Add the flour and baking powder, and beat slowly, only until the batter is homogenous. Spread half of the batter in one pan.

To add to the chocolate cake, melt the cocoa powder and chocolate-milk mix in the boiling water, add to the remaining batter in the mixer, and mix at low speed, until the cocoa mixture is incorporated and the batter is chocolate brown. Spread the dark batter in the other pan.

Bake the cakes for 35 minutes, until a toothpick inserted in their centers comes out dry. Let cool completely.

Release the cakes from the pans, and level their tops with a knife. Slice each cake horizontally, to get 2 even disks (you will have 2 vanilla disks and 2 chocolate ones). Place the four layers on your work surface. Center an upside-down 6-inch (15-cm) bowl on each layer, and cut around it. Now center an upside-down 3-inch (7.5-cm) cup on each layer, and cut around it. Each disk is now cut into 3 different size circles. Separate all the cutout circles and reassemble them, so that in each layer the inner and outer circles are the same color, while the second (middle) circle is the opposite color.

To make the chocolate filling, mix the chocolate spread and boiling water to a soft, spreadable cream.

On a large serving platter, place a white-black-white layer (this must be done carefully, preferably with four hands, but if it breaks a little en route to the platter, that's not too bad). Spread a thin layer of the chocolate filling and place a black-white-black layer on top. Repeat with the next two layers, alternating white-black-white and black-white-black, and spreading chocolate between the layers. The last layer will be black-white-black, and does not need chocolate spread on it.

To make the frosting, in a mixer, beat together the whipping cream, milk and pudding mix until firm peaks form. Frost the cake on top and around the sides.

Serve the cake whole, cut the first slice, pull it out, and . . . whoosh! . . . a gasp of admiration and a standing ovation! Take a bow!

Keep covered in the refrigerator.

Center an upside-down 6-inch (15-cm) bowl on each layer, and cut around it.

Center an upside-down 3-inch (7.5-cm) cup on each layer, and cut around it.

Separate all the cutout circles.

Reassemble circles, so that in each layer the middle circle is the opposite color.

Spread each circle with a thin layer of the chocolate filling.

Stack circles, alternating white-black-white and black-white-black.

Make the frosting and frost the cake on top . . .

. . . and around the sides.

Medovik (Layers of Honey, Sour Cream and Crumbs)

As a child, I knew this cake as the "schmeten torte," but it's better known by its Russian name, medovik (and I dare not enter the debate about which region of the Soviet Union it originally came from). The medovik is made with honey, short-crust pastry and sour cream filling. This beauty, however, comes with a very serious warning: Do not touch it for 24 hours after baking; it needs its beauty sleep in the refrigerator, until the filling softens the pastry, and it turns from crispy to melt-in-your-mouth. Finally, the long wait is awarded: a soft, creamy, sweet and sour creation that you just can't stop "trimming."

ONE 10-INCH (25-CM) CAKE

FOR THE DOUGH

3 eggs, at room temperature

1 cup (200g) sugar

3½ oz (100g) butter, diced

½ cup (120ml) honey

Zest of ½ orange

4 cups (560g) all-purpose flour, plus more for rolling

1 tbsp (10g) baking powder

FOR THE SOUR CREAM FILLING

5 cups (1200ml) full-fat sour cream

¾ cup (150g) sugar

1 tsp vanilla extract

GRANDMA KNOWS BEST

The sour cream with 27 percent fat is perfect for this cake, because it is thicker than the regular 15 percent variety. Be warned that if you do use the 15 percent sour cream, the filling will be a little runny, which means you will have to assemble the cake in a sealed pan and not directly on the serving platter.

To make the dough, in a mixer fitted with the whisk attachment, beat the eggs and sugar at high speed for 10 minutes, until the mixture is fluffy and thick like a mousse.

In a microwave oven, melt the butter and honey. Lower the mixer's speed, and add the honey mixture and the orange zest, while beating.

Replace the whisk attachment with a flat one, add the flour and baking powder, and mix only until the dough is homogenous, soft and sticky.

Line a plastic container or a small pan with plastic wrap, and grease the wrap. Spread the dough in the container (or pan), cover with another greased sheet of plastic wrap and put in the refrigerator for 4 hours to set.

To make the sour cream filling, in a bowl, mix together the sour cream, sugar and vanilla. Wait 5 minutes for the sugar to dissolve, and whisk until smooth.

Keep in the refrigerator to set.

In the meantime, bake the cake's bases. Preheat the oven to 325°F (160°C).

Divide the dough into 6 equal parts. On parchment paper generously dusted with flour, roll each part into a 10-inch (25-cm) circle (use a ring or a plate to get a precise circle of dough). Do not skimp on flouring your work surface, or rolling will be a very sticky experience.

With the paper it was rolled on, place each dough circle on a separate baking sheet and bake for 15 minutes, until golden. You'll probably have to do it in rotations, unless you happen to have six baking sheets and two ovens. Set aside to cool.

In a food processor, shred one of the bases (the "ugliest," preferably) into crumbs.

Place a baked base on a large, flat serving platter. Spread with the filling. Cover with another base and spread with filling. Continue stacking base layers, covering each one with filling, until you have assembled all 5 layers of cake and filling (the top layer will be filling). Spread the remaining filling around the sides of the cake as frosting. Sprinkle the crumbs all over the cake. Be gentle, as the sour cream frosting has not set yet (don't worry, it will set beautifully in the refrigerator).

Cover the cake and transfer it to the refrigerator for 24 hours. It's a must! Don't even taste it before, or you will be sorely disappointed. After 24 hours, serve it cold, straight from the refrigerator, and enjoy.

The Bee Sting

When my parents exhaust the weekly supply of my cakes, they pop over to my good friend Mickey Shemo's pastry shop and stock up on sweets. Among Mickey's creations, their favorite, the one they absolutely swoon over, is his Bee Sting Cake, a yeast cake filled with vanilla cream and coated with almonds and honey.

When I tried to re-create this nostalgic recipe for my book, I ran into a problem: The cake was great on the day it was baked, but a few hours in the refrigerator dried it up. I called Mickey, complimented him profusely, then popped the question. "How come my Bee Sting dries up so quickly while yours stays moist and moist for days?" Mickey was only too happy to share his sweet secret—wetting the cake with a honey syrup after baking. Thank you, Mickey; now my cake can also be swooned over!

ONE 10-INCH (25-CM) CAKE

FOR THE YEAST DOUGH
2½ cups (350g) all-purpose flour

1 tbsp (8g) active dry yeast

3½ oz (100g) butter, diced

½ cup (120ml) milk

¼ cup (50g) sugar

2 eggs

FOR THE ALMONDS AND HONEY COATING
½ cup (100g) sugar

¼ cup (60ml) honey

3½ oz (100g) butter

¼ cup (60ml) whipping cream

1 cup (100g) sliced almonds

FOR THE VANILLA CREAM FILLING
2 cups (480ml) whipping cream

1 cup (240ml) milk

½ cup (80g) vanilla-flavored instant pudding mix

¼ cup (50g) sugar

FOR THE SYRUP
2 heaping tbsp (30ml) honey

¾ cup (180ml) boiling water

To make the dough, in a mixer fitted with the kneading attachment, combine the flour and yeast.

In a microwave oven, melt the butter and stir in the milk, to make a lukewarm mixture. Add to the mixer along with the sugar and eggs, and mix for 5 minutes at medium speed, until the dough is smooth and very sticky.

Line a 10-inch (25-cm) springform pan with a circle of parchment paper. With wet hands, flatten the dough into the prepared pan (the dough will reach only about one-third of the pan's height, but that's okay). Cover and let rise, until it doubles in bulk, 1–2 hours.

In the meantime, make the almonds and honey coating. In a pot (make sure it is not too small, as the mixture rises when boiling) over medium heat, heat the sugar, honey, butter and whipping cream. Let the mixture boil for 2 minutes, then remove from the stove and mix in the sliced almonds. Let cool a little.

In the meantime, preheat the oven to 350°F (180°C).

Spread the now lukewarm almond-honey coating over the dough in the pan (do it gently so as not to let the air out of the risen dough). Bake for 20–25 minutes, until the coating bubbles and the dough is golden (carefully insert the tip of a knife through the coating, move it a little to see the interior, and make sure it is not "doughy"). Remove from the oven and let cool completely.

To make the filling, in a mixer, beat the whipping cream, milk, pudding mix and sugar to a homogenous cream.

To make the syrup, stir the honey into the boiling until the honey is dissolved.

Release the cake from the pan. With a serrated bread knife, cut the cake horizontally to get 2 equal layers. Put the first (bottom) layer on a serving platter and wet it with half of the syrup (do it with a spoon, and make sure you cover the whole surface). Spread the filling (all of it) over the first layer. Put the top layer of cake upside down (the almond coating facing down) on a board, and wet it with the remaining syrup. Turn it back over (the coating facing up), and cut into 12 equal triangles (for easier slicing later on). Arrange the triangles (with the almond coating facing up) close together on the layer of filling. Keep in the refrigerator, and serve cold.

Vanilla Roulade Filled with Strawberry Jam and Whipped Cream

Grandmothers can make this roulade "in their sleep." It is a thin sponge, baked in a flat tray, filled with jam and whipped cream and rolled up. This is an especially good recipe; the cake is very soft, and it doesn't crack (well, hardly at all) when rolled, so you don't have to pre-roll it in a towel like they used to do. I do, however, cover it with a thick towel after baking until it is cold—a little dryness-preventing tip.

ONE 15½-INCH (40-CM) LONG CAKE

FOR THE VANILLA SPONGE

Powdered sugar, for dusting the pan and for serving

4 eggs, separated

¾ cup (150g) granulated sugar

1 tsp vanilla extract

Zest of ½ lemon

½ cup (70g) all-purpose flour

2 tbsp (20g) cornstarch

1 tbsp (15ml) vegetable oil

FOR THE WHIPPED CREAM AND JAM FILLING

1 cup (240ml) whipping cream

2 tbsp (20g) powdered sugar

1 cup (240g) strawberry jam

GRANDMA KNOWS BEST

Too lazy to separate the eggs? You can make the easier (slightly less fluffy, but still soft and yummy) roulade: Beat whole eggs with sugar at high speed for 10 minutes, add the rest of the ingredients from the original recipe plus 1 teaspoon baking powder, and slowly beat until combined. Baking is the same.

To make the sponge cake, preheat the oven to 350°F (180°C). Line an 11½ x 15½-inch (30 x 40-cm) oven tray with parchment paper, grease the paper and dust with a little powdered sugar.

In a mixer, beat the egg whites at medium speed for 1 minute, until they form a white froth with large bubbles. Gradually add the granulated sugar while beating, until the meringue is firm and shiny. Lower the mixer's speed to minimum, add the egg yolks, vanilla and lemon zest, and slowly beat until combined. Add the flour and cornstarch and slowly beat, only until combined and all lumps are smoothed out. Add the oil and beat only until combined.

Spread the batter in the prepared baking tray and bake for 15 minutes, until the cake is soft and springy to the touch and a toothpick inserted in its center comes out dry.

On your work surface, lay another sheet of parchment paper, and dust it with powdered sugar. Take the cake out of the oven and flip it (with the paper it was baked on) over the new, sugar-dusted parchment paper (if the sides of the cake are stuck to the pan, use a knife to release them before you turn the cake over). Let the cake cool under a thick towel.

To make the filling, in a mixer, beat the whipping cream and powdered sugar to firm peaks.

Peel off the parchment paper the cake was baked on. Spread strawberry jam on the cake followed by an even layer of the whipped cream, leaving a 1-inch (2.5-cm) margin on all sides, to ensure easy and neat rolling. Using the paper under the cake, roll it into a roulade. Don't worry if the roulade cracks a little; it will still come out gorgeous.

Transfer the roulade to the refrigerator for 2 hours to set. Dust the roulade with powdered sugar, and bring it whole to the table. Slice and serve. Keep covered in the refrigerator, and serve cold.

orgeous Chocolate-Mocha Roulade

A soft chocolate cake "hugging" a coffee-flavored whipped cream, all covered by chocolate ganache. One bite of this creation and you are on cloud nine. With no flour, this cake is good for gluten intolerance as well as being a great and festive dessert option for Passover (for a nondairy version, simply substitute the dairy whipping cream with a nondairy one).

ONE 15½-INCH (40-CM) LONG CAKE

FOR THE CHOCOLATE CAKE
¼ cup (40g) cocoa powder, plus more for dusting the pan

5 eggs, separated, at room temperature

½ cup (100g) sugar

1 tsp vanilla extract

2 tbsp (20g) cornstarch

FOR THE COFFEE-FLAVORED WHIPPED CREAM FILLING
1 cup (240ml) whipping cream

2 tsp (8g) instant coffee powder

¼ cup (50g) sugar

FOR THE GANACHE FROSTING
½ cup (120ml) whipping cream

4 oz (120g) dark chocolate

GRANDMA KNOWS BEST
If you choose to spread a little Nutella on the cake before you spread with the coffee filling, you will hear no complaints from me, but if you do it, I suggest you dilute the Nutella paste (3 tablespoons [45ml] boiling water to 1 cup [250g] paste) so it will spread easily and not tear the delicate cake.

To make the chocolate cake, preheat the oven to 350°F (180°C). Line an 11½ x 15½-inch (30 x 40-cm) baking tray with parchment paper, grease the paper and dust it with cocoa powder.

In a mixer, beat the egg whites at medium speed for 1 minute, until they form a white froth with large bubbles. Gradually add the sugar 1 tablespoon (12g) at a time, at 10-second intervals, while beating. When all the sugar is incorporated, beat for another minute, until the meringue is firm and shiny.

Add the egg yolks and vanilla, and slowly beat until combined. Sift in the cocoa powder and cornstarch, and slowly beat until combined.

Spread the batter in the baking tray, and bake for 15 minutes, until the cake is soft and springy to the touch and a toothpick inserted in its center comes out dry.

On your work surface, lay another sheet of parchment paper, and dust it with cocoa powder. Take the cake out of the oven and flip it (with the paper it was baked on) over the new, cocoa-dusted parchment paper (if the sides of the cake are stuck to the pan, use a knife to release them before you turn the cake over). Let the cake cool under a thick kitchen towel.

To make the coffee-flavored whipped cream, in a mixer, beat the whipping cream, instant coffee powder and sugar to firm peaks.

Peel off the original sheet of parchment paper (the one the cake was baked on). Spread the whipped cream on the cake, leaving a 1-inch (2.5-cm) margin on all sides, for easy and neat rolling. Using the paper under the cake, roll it into a roulade. Don't worry if the roulade cracks a little; it will still come out gorgeous. Transfer the roulade to the freezer for 1–2 hours to set.

To make the chocolate ganache, in a microwave oven, heat the whipping cream and chocolate. Whisk to a smooth sauce.

Pour the chocolate frosting over the roulade, letting it drizzle down the sides and cover the whole cake. For a clean and neat result, I recommend you line the serving tray with strips of parchment paper that can be pulled out from under the cake after frosting. Keep in the refrigerator until you are ready to serve. Slice with a knife dipped in boiling water.

Three-Layer Cheesecake

Only six ingredients are required for this intricate, three-layer creation of sponge, cheese and meringue. For simpler, foolproof execution, this recipe is written slightly differently. Read the instructions carefully and adhere to them religiously, and your success is guaranteed. Made properly, this cake is really mind-blowing.

ONE 10-INCH (25-CM) CAKE

8 eggs, at room temperature

1½ cups (300g) sugar, divided

¾ cup (100g) all-purpose flour

2 cups (500g) cream cheese

1 cup (250g) Greek yogurt

½ cup (80g) vanilla-flavored instant pudding mix, divided

Preheat the oven to 350°F (180°C). Grease a 10-inch (25-cm) springform pan.

In a mixer, beat 5 of the eggs and ¾ cup (150g) of the sugar for 10 minutes at high speed, until the mixture is fluffy and thick like mousse. Add the flour and beat slowly, until combined.

Pour half of the batter into the prepared pan (keep the other half in the bowl for later), and bake for 15 minutes, until the cake is golden and springy to the touch. Take out of the oven, and let cool a little. Lower the oven's temperature to 325°F (160°C) and leave it on.

Separate the remaining 3 eggs. Add the 3 yolks, cream cheese, yogurt and ¼ cup (40g) of the pudding mix to the remaining batter in the bowl, and gently whisk until smooth. Pour the cheese mixture over the baked base.

Bake for 30 minutes, until the filling starts to set. Take out of the oven (leaving it on), and prepare the meringue.

In a clean and dry mixer bowl, beat the remaining 3 egg whites at medium speed for 1 minute. Gradually (1 tablespoon [12g] at a time, at 10-second intervals) add the remaining ¾ cup (150g) sugar, and go on beating for 2 more minutes after all the sugar is added, until the meringue is shiny and creamy. Add the remaining ¼ cup (40g) pudding mix, and slowly mix until combined.

Transfer the meringue to a piping bag with a wide, smooth tip, and pipe a spiral of meringue over the cake, starting in the center and going out toward the edges in a circular motion, until the entire cake is covered.

Return the pan to the oven for 20 minutes and bake until the meringue is golden. Cool completely before slicing and serving. Keep in the refrigerator.

GRANDMA KNOWS BEST

It is better to pipe the meringue than spread it, because the cake is very delicate and might break. Piping can be done in any way you like ("kisses," strips, spirals— you name it), as long as the meringue layer is plump and thick, using the entire amount of meringue—you don't want any leftover meringue in the piping bag.

Who Doesn't Love This Cheesecake

My friend's father, Mr. Haim Gueta, has a weird food obsession: He won't eat anything white, especially cheese in any way, shape or form (he even eats his pizza without the cheese). Except . . . except this cake! He doesn't eat it, he devours it, and so do the rest of his family, and the rest of the world for that matter; I am yet to meet someone who doesn't like this cake. This baked cheesecake has more air in it than actual cheese; it is so airy, I don't know what holds it together. As far as the nostalgia factor is concerned, if I were asked to rate the recipes in this book according to their nostalgia-ness, this one would definitely be among the top five.

ONE 13 X 11-INCH (33 X 28-CM) CAKE

FOR THE CAKE
2 cups (500g) cream cheese

1 cup (250g) Greek yogurt

¾ cup (200ml) sour cream

6 eggs, separated

1 cup (200g) sugar, divided

¼ cup (40g) vanilla-flavored instant pudding mix

½ cup (70g) cornstarch

FOR THE CREAM
2 cups (480ml) whipping cream

¼ cup (40g) vanilla-flavored instant pudding mix

¼ cup (50g) sugar

2 oz (50g) dark or milk chocolate

To make the cake, preheat the oven to 325°F (160°C). Put a deep pan on the oven's floor and fill it with 2 inches (5cm) of boiling water. Grease a 13 x 11-inch (33 x 28-cm) pan well on both the sides and the bottom.

In the largest bowl in the house, whisk together the cream cheese, yogurt, sour cream, egg yolks, ½ cup (100g) of the sugar, pudding mix and cornstarch to a homogenous mixture.

In a mixer, beat the egg whites at medium speed, until they turn into a soft white froth. Gradually add the remaining ½ cup (100g) sugar, and beat until the meringue is shiny and creamy. Whisk one-third of the meringue into the cheese mixture. Gently fold in the remaining meringue, only until the batter is homogenous and fluffy. Spread the batter in the prepared pan. Bake for 50–60 minutes. The cake is ready when it is brown and springy, has risen very high, is firm to the touch and a toothpick inserted in its center comes out clean. Take the cake out of the oven, and let it cool completely. The cake will lose some of its height, but that's okay.

To make the cream, in a mixer, beat the whipping cream with the pudding mix and sugar to soft peaks. Spread the cream on the cooled cake, and grate the chocolate over it for garnish.

Transfer the cake to the refrigerator for at least 4 hours to cool and set. Serve cold. Keep covered in the refrigerator.

GRANDMA KNOWS BEST

This cake is so delicate and airy that if you bake it without the bath of boiling water, ugly cracks will appear. By "bath" I mean a real sauna—with two full kettles of boiling water poured into the pan. Thanks to this steamy environment, we don't have to go through a double-bake (high heat followed by low heat) process anymore. Until I discovered this steam "sauna" effect, I used to cover up the shame with a lot of whipped cream.

This cake rises a lot during baking, and goes back to its original height when cooled. To allow this rising and falling process, it is important to make sure the sides of the cake are not stuck to the wall of the pan (or it would tear and crack). This is why I grease the walls as well as the bottom of the pan. If, during baking, you detect any sticking, carefully open the oven, wait a few seconds for the steam to subside and pass a knife between the cake and the pan.

Melt-in-Your-Mouth Cheesecake with Sour Cream Frosting

Eyeball the list of ingredients here—looks like a regular cheesecake, right? Wrong! This is an insanely rich and creamy cheesecake, thanks to the hot-water-bath baking technique. The cake sits in its "hot tub" for almost 2 hours (make sure you don't forget to seal the cake pan before you pour the batter in, by tightly wrapping it with aluminum foil on the outside). As it is, this cake is so tall and creamy that I didn't add a short-crust base to the recipe—it is all cheese (well . . . apart from the time-honored sour cream frosting), and that's the magic of it.

ONE 10-INCH (25-CM) CAKE

FOR THE CAKE
3 cups (700g) cream cheese
1½ cups (350g) Greek yogurt
1¼ cups (300ml) sour cream
1½ cups (300g) sugar, divided
3 tbsp (45 ml) vanilla extract
6 eggs, separated
¾ cup (100g) cornstarch

FOR THE SOUR CREAM FROSTING
1¼ cups (300ml) sour cream
3 tbsp (30g) sugar
½ tsp vanilla extract

GRANDMA KNOWS BEST

Back in the day, it was customary to return the cake to the oven for a few minutes after the cake was frosted with the sour cream, so the frosting would be shiny and extra smooth. However, I discovered a shortcut, rendering this step unnecessary—I simply heat the frosting in the microwave oven, until it is shiny and smooth, and only then spread it over the cold cake.

To make the cake, preheat the oven to 300°F (150°C). Generously grease the bottom and sides of a 10-inch (25-cm) springform pan, and tightly wrap it with aluminum foil on the outside (so the water from the "bath" will not infiltrate into the cake itself during baking).

Place a deep pan in the center of the oven's floor, and fill it to half its height with boiling water (about 2 full kettles).

In the largest bowl in the house, whisk together the cream cheese, yogurt, sour cream, ¾ cup (150g) of the sugar, vanilla and egg yolks. Add the cornstarch and whisk vigorously for 1 minute, until all lumps are dissolved and the mixture is smooth and homogenous.

In a mixer, beat the egg whites at medium speed, until they turn to a soft white froth. Gradually add the remaining ¾ cup (150g) sugar, and beat until the meringue is shiny and creamy. Whisk one-third of the meringue into the cheese mixture. Gently fold the remaining meringue in, only until the batter is smooth and fluffy.

Spread the batter in the prepared pan. Carefully place the pan in the bath of boiling water (add more boiling water if necessary—the water should reach three-fourths of the cake pan's height). Bake for 1 hour and 45 minutes, until the cake is very brown, very tall and springy and firm to the touch.

Turn off the oven, open its door all the way and leave the baked cake in the turned-off, open oven for another ½ hour (the main reason for this is to let the boiling water cool, so you won't burn yourself when you take it out).

Carefully take the cake out of the "bath" and out of the oven, and set to cool at room temperature. The cake will go back to the height of the pan during the cooling process, and that's okay.

To make the frosting, in a microwave-safe bowl, mix together the sour cream, sugar and vanilla. Heat for 1 minute in a microwave oven, until all the sugar has dissolved and the frosting is warm, runny and shiny. Spread immediately over the cake.

Transfer to the refrigerator for 4 hours to cool and set. Serve cold. Keep covered in the refrigerator.

Gugelhupf (Yeast Sponge)

I swear to you—I did try to cut corners: I mixed all the ingredients, let it rise and baked it. The cake was good but not great. If this cake is to be anything like the legendary grandma gugelhupf, if we want the perfect airy consistency, it must have its three risings. Let your gugelhupf rise three times, and you will not regret it! Just wait until this beauty comes out of the oven!

ONE 9½-INCH (24-CM) CAKE

FOR THE YEAST STARTER

2 tsp (7g) active dry yeast

½ cup (120ml) lukewarm water

1 tbsp (15ml) honey

1 cup (140g) all-purpose flour

FOR THE DOUGH

3½ oz (100g) butter

½ cup (120ml) milk

½ cup (100g) granulated sugar, plus more for sprinkling

1 egg

Zest of ½ lemon

1 tsp vanilla extract

1 tsp salt

2 cups (280g) all-purpose flour

FOR THE CAKE ADD-INS

1 cup (150g) raisins

¼ cup (60ml) rum or water

¼ cup (25g) peeled almonds, for garnish

Powdered sugar, for serving

To make the starter, in a mixer fitted with the kneading attachment, combine the yeast and water. Add the honey and flour. Mix for 2 minutes at medium speed, until homogenous. Cover and let rise, until the batter is full of bubbles and almost doubled in bulk, about ½ hour.

To make the dough, in a microwave oven, melt the butter. Add the milk and stir to a lukewarm mixture.

Add the milk mixture to the batter in the mixer bowl. Add the sugar, egg, lemon zest, vanilla, salt and flour, and knead for 10 minutes, until the dough is smooth, shiny and very sticky. Cover the bowl, and let the dough rise until doubled in bulk, about 1 hour.

In the meantime, grease a 9½-inch (24-cm) Bundt pan and sprinkle with granulated sugar to prevent sticking.

To make the cake add-ins, combine the raisins and rum in a microwave-safe bowl and heat for 30 seconds in a microwave oven, to make them moist. Set aside to cool. Put whole almonds on the bottom of the prepared pan.

Add the raisins and the residual rum to the dough in the bowl, and, using a spatula (to distribute the raisins evenly, and to let out the air), fold them in.

Gently spread the dough over the almonds in the pan—it should come up to half the pan's height. Cover and let rise, until the dough doubles in bulk and reaches the top rim of the pan (this takes longer than usual—about 2 hours).

Toward the end of the last rising period, preheat the oven to 350°F (180°C).

Put the cake in the oven, and bake for 40 minutes, until golden and firm. Let the cake cool a little, and turn it over on a rack to cool all the way through. Dust with powdered sugar, and serve.

GRANDMA KNOWS BEST

Here's a great tip to restore the moistness of the cake after a day or two: Brush it with a sugar syrup (made by boiling ½ cup [100g] sugar and ½ cup [120ml] water for 2 minutes).

Aunt Linda's Mind-Blowing Yeast Roulade

How I tried and tried to re-create my Aunt Linda's yeast cake! Aunt Linda is a master baker whose recipe notebook was lost when she moved to Colombia (I miss her so much!). Aunt Linda did not remember the recipe by heart, so, with the help of my beautiful cousin Maya, who is a talented baker herself, we set out on a quest to discover the lost cake. We asked Aunt Maggie and Uncle Danny; we interrogated Aunt Lilly and pestered Aunt Anatie; we even located "Miss Sarit," Maya's junior-high teacher, who was rumored to be in possession of the recipe. I am telling you—we didn't leave one stone unturned. Throughout this journey, we managed to uncover bits and pieces, which, when joined together, completed the puzzle. We re-created Aunt Linda's yeast roulade, and—yes, it is mind-blowing! The dough is so soft and velvety, you want to curl up in it and go to sleep . . . but you won't, because you just can't stop eating it. I like to crowd the roulades together tightly in a deep oven tray. They are joined, and it is so much fun tearing them apart with your hands. If, however, you go for a more professional look, especially if you intend to give it a gift, I suggest you bake them in individual loaf pans.

4 ROULADES

FOR THE YEAST STARTER

1 cup (240ml) lukewarm water

2 tbsp (17g) active dry yeast

1 tbsp (12g) sugar

FOR THE DOUGH

14 oz (400g) butter-flavored margarine

1 cup (240ml) milk

10 tbsp (130g) sugar

1 tsp salt

2 eggs

7 cups (1kg) all-purpose flour, plus more for dusting

FOR THE FILLING

4 cups (1kg) chocolate spread

½ cup (80g) chocolate-milk mix

FOR THE GLAZE

½ cup (120ml) milk

½ cup (100g) sugar

1 tsp vanilla extract

GRANDMA KNOWS BEST

I always make this dough with margarine; it causes the cakes to stay moist longer.

To make the yeast starter, in a bowl, combine the lukewarm water, yeast and sugar. Set aside for 10 minutes to develop, until froth forms on top.

To make the dough, in a microwave-safe bowl, melt the margarine in a microwave oven, add the milk and stir to get a lukewarm mixture. Transfer to a mixer fitted with the kneading attachment, and add the sugar, salt, eggs and the yeast mixture. Knead at medium speed, gradually adding the flour 1 cup (140g) every 10 seconds or so. Keep kneading for another 2–3 minutes after all the flour has been incorporated, until the dough is shiny, velvety and very soft (it is going to be a little runny, but that's okay, it will set in the refrigerator). Cover and transfer to the refrigerator for 4 hours to rise and set.

Transfer the dough to a work surface dusted with flour. Divide into 8 equal parts (the easiest way to achieve this is to flatten the dough into a circular shape and cut it like a pizza into 8 equal triangles). Roll each part into a rectangle, just under ½-inch (1.3-cm) thick.

To make the filling, spread with ½ cup (125g) of the chocolate spread, sprinkle with 1 tablespoon (10g) chocolate-milk mix and roll into a roulade. Twist together every two roulades (screw-like).

Line a deep baking tray with parchment paper. Place the 4 coiled cakes in the pan. Cover with plastic wrap and set aside for 30 minutes for partial rising (the cakes are not supposed to double in bulk this time, because most of the rising occurs in the oven).

Toward the end of the rising stage, preheat the oven to 350°F (180°C).

Bake the roulades (without an egg glazing) for 30–35 minutes, until the cakes have risen and joined, and they are brown and fragrant (they are not shiny at this stage, but don't worry—the sweet milk will take care of that later).

To make the glaze, in a small pot or a microwave oven, bring the milk almost to a boil. Mix in the sugar and vanilla, and whisk until dissolved. Brush the hot glaze on the hot cakes immediately upon taking them out of the oven.

Let cool a little, and gently pull them apart. I dare not tell you to wait until the cakes have cooled completely, because if you are anything like me, you will devour them hot. Yummy!

Babka—Just as It Should Be

Here are a few things that set the babka (a chocolate yeast cake with crumbs) apart:

- The dough is rolled out very thin, which guarantees many swirls of dough and chocolate.
- The filling has two flavors: cocoa and cinnamon.
- The cake has short-crust pastry crumbs (streusel).
- It has a special design—the roulade is folded in half and twisted.
- It has a very short second rising; no doubling of bulk is necessary.
- The cake is glazed with egg white to help the streusel stick.
- The cake is baked until dark brown (covered with aluminum foil to prevent burning).

2 LOAF CAKES

FOR THE DOUGH

4½ cups (630g) all-purpose flour, plus more for dusting

1 tbsp (8g) active dry yeast

½ cup (100g) sugar

1 cup (240ml) lukewarm milk

2 eggs + 1 egg yolk (save the white for the glaze)

½ tsp salt

5 oz (150g) butter, very soft

FOR THE COCOA AND CINNAMON FILLING

2 cups (400g) sugar

1 tsp vanilla extract

1 tbsp (6g) ground cinnamon

½ cup (70g) cocoa powder

3½ oz (100g) butter, melted and lukewarm

FOR THE STREUSEL

3½ tbsp (50g) cold butter, diced

⅓ cup (70g) sugar

½ cup (70g) all-purpose flour

FOR THE GLAZE

1 egg white

To make the dough, in a mixer fitted with the kneading attachment, combine the flour and yeast. Add the sugar, milk, 2 whole eggs, 1 egg yolk, salt and butter, and knead together for 5 minutes at medium speed, until the dough is smooth, wrapped around the kneading attachment and sticks to the bottom of the mixer bowl. Cover the bowl with plastic wrap and set aside to rise, until the dough doubles in bulk, 1–2 hours.

To make the filling, in a mixing bowl, combine the sugar, vanilla, cinnamon and cocoa, and set aside.

Lightly dust your work surface with flour, transfer the dough from the mixer bowl to the work surface, and divide it in half. Working with each half separately, roll it out as thinly as you can (about ⅛ inch [3mm]) into a large rectangle about 14 x 24 inches (35.5 x 60.5cm). If the dough sticks to the surface, lift it and dust with flour again.

Spread half of the melted butter on the rolled-out dough. Sprinkle with half of the filling mixture. Roll the dough up into a roulade (be very patient—the dough is very thin and you want there to be as many swirls as possible). Fold the roulade in half (like the letter U) and twist it around itself like a screw. Repeat the rolling out, filling, folding and twisting with the other half of the dough, filling and melted butter.

Grease 2 loaf pans or line with parchment paper. Transfer the cakes to the pans and set aside for ½ hour to "rest" (in the summer, 20 minutes should be enough). The cakes are supposed to rise just a little; they definitely won't double in bulk.

In the meantime, make the streusel. In a bowl, combine the butter, sugar and flour, and break with your fingers, until the mixture is flaky with uneven crumbs (some large, some small—that's the beauty of it). Keep in the refrigerator.

Preheat the oven to 350°F (180°C).

To make the glaze, with a fork, whisk the egg white for about 1 minute, until it foams up a little. Gently brush the cakes with it. Sprinkle half the streusel on each cake.

Bake for 25 minutes, until the cakes have browned. Remove from the oven and loosely cover each one with aluminum foil. Lower the oven temperature to 325°F (160°C) and return the cakes to bake for another 20 minutes (total baking time is 45 minutes). The cakes are ready when they are dark brown and you can no longer resist the aroma in your kitchen. Cool a little before slicing and eating. Keep covered at room temperature (they also freeze very well).

Fold-Up Yeast Cake

This yeast cake has the longest "life span" I know—it stays fresh and tasty for four (4!) days. The secret to its moistness (and special look) is in the rolling of the filling into the dough. It requires a little more design work compared to other yeast cakes, but it is worth it—you will understand what I mean when you have taken the first bite.

3 LOAF CAKES

FOR THE DOUGH

5 cups (700g) all-purpose flour, plus more for dusting

1 tbsp (8g) active dry yeast

7 oz (200g) butter

1 cup (240ml) milk

½ cup (100g) sugar

3 eggs

½ tsp salt

FOR THE FILLING

Your favorite chocolate spread (about 2 cups [500g])

Dulce de leche (about 1½ cups [375g])

FOR THE GLAZE

1 egg, whisked with 1 tbsp (15ml) water

GRANDMA KNOWS BEST

In this recipe, you spread filling twice. I like the combination of chocolate and dulce de leche, but you can choose to use chocolate both times or substitute the dulce de leche with nougat, peanut butter, date paste, halva spread or even raw tahini.

To make the dough, in a mixer fitted with the kneading attachment, combine the flour and yeast. In a microwave oven, melt the butter, then stir in the milk to a lukewarm mixture. Add to the mixer bowl along with the sugar, eggs and salt, and knead for 2–3 minutes, only until the dough is smooth and shiny. Cover, and set aside to rise until doubled in bulk, 1–2 hours. Transfer the risen dough to a floured work surface, and divide into 3 equal parts. Working with each part separately, roll out to a roughly 10 x 12-inch (25 x 30.5-cm) rectangle.

For the filling, generously spread the dough with the chocolate spread, leaving a 1-inch (2.5-cm) margin all around. Fold the right-hand side third over the middle third of the dough. Now, fold the left-hand side third to cover the folded parts, like folding a letter. Turn the folded dough 90 degrees, and roll it again into a 10 x 12-inch (25 x 30.5-cm) rectangle, dusting with flour as needed. The dough should be just under ½ inch (1.3cm) thick (don't worry if the filling "peeps" out a little, just keep flouring and rolling).

Spread the folded and re-rolled dough with a generous layer of dulce de leche.

Repeat the folding by thirds, but this time do not roll it out again. Cut the dough into 3 strips and braid it. Repeat with the remaining dough. Grease 3 loaf pans. Place the "braids" in the greased loaf pans, and set aside to rise for 20 minutes (the cakes will not double in bulk, and that's okay). Preheat the oven to 350°F (180°C).

For the glaze, gently brush each braid with the egg. Bake for 35–40 minutes, until golden. Cool a little, and serve (I like to dust the cakes with powdered sugar and drizzle strips of melted dark chocolate, as shown in the photo). Keep at room temperature.

Spread the (folded and re-rolled) dough with filling and fold by thirds.

Cut the dough into 3 strips.

Braid the dough and place in a greased loaf pan.

Old-Days Yeast Krantz

This krantz is made with a special yeast dough, called "yeast-raised short-crust dough." This dough does not rise like the regular krantz, and the cake stays dense and crispy. It goes very well with a special date and chocolate filling I make, but you can use any filling you like (even the chocolate spread is great in it). And don't let the quantity of butter in the recipe intimidate you; bear in mind that you get three (3!) beautiful large cakes out of it, so as long as you can limit yourself to one or two slices of this great cake, you are "safe." If only there was a slimming way to eat the cake and keep the waistline, too . . .

3 CAKES

FOR THE YEAST STARTER
½ cup (120ml) lukewarm milk
1 tsp granulated sugar
1 tbsp (8g) active dry yeast

FOR THE DOUGH
4 cups (560g) all-purpose flour, plus more for dusting
⅓ cup (70g) granulated sugar
7 oz (200g) butter or margarine, softened
3 egg yolks
¾ cup (200ml) sour cream
½ tsp salt

FOR THE FILLING
4 tbsp (40g) cocoa powder
½ cup (100g) granulated sugar
4 tbsp (160g) date paste
7 oz (200g) butter or margarine, softened
½ tsp ground cinnamon

FOR THE GLAZE
¾ cup (100g) powdered sugar
2 tbsp (30ml) milk
½ tsp vanilla extract

To make the yeast starter, in a cup, combine the lukewarm milk, sugar and yeast. Set aside for 10 minutes, until dissolved.

To make the dough, in a mixer fitted with the flat attachment, combine the flour, granulated sugar and butter and beat at medium speed for 2 minutes, to a crumbly consistency. Lower the mixer's speed and add the yeast mixture, egg yolks, sour cream and salt, and mix for another minute, to get a homogenous, soft and not sticky dough (this dough does not require long kneading like a regular yeast dough). Cover the mixer bowl with plastic wrap and put in the refrigerator for at least 2 hours (and up to 12). The dough will hardly rise at all, and that's okay.

To make the filling, combine all the filling ingredients together to form a homogenous mixture. Set aside. Preheat the oven to 350°F (180°C). Line a baking sheet with parchment paper.

Transfer the cold dough onto a floured work surface, and divide it into 3 equal parts (work with each part individually, and keep the other parts in the refrigerator, so they don't warm up and soften). Roll each part into a thin rectangle, spread with one-third of the filling and roll into a roulade. Flatten the roulade a little with your hands (it is easier to cut this way). Cut each roulade in half lengthwise to get 2 strips attached at one end. Twist the two strips like a screw, with the filling turned upward and showing. Place the roulades spaciously on the prepared baking sheet and bake immediately, without another rising, for 25–30 minutes, until the cakes are brown and fragrant.

To make the glaze, in a small microwave-safe bowl, combine the powdered sugar, milk and vanilla to a smooth paste. Heat in the microwave oven for 20–30 seconds, until soft and runny.

With a teaspoon, using a back-and-forth motion, drizzle strips of glaze quite close together. The glaze will set at room temperature in about 30 minutes, but if you can't wait that long, well—these cakes are great hot, warm and at room temperature.

Poppy Seed Roulade ("Pressburger")

What is a "burger" doing in a poppy seed cake? The Pressburger is a poppy seed–filled yeast pastry, named after the capital of Slovakia—Pressburg (today's Bratislava). Originally, it is a stuffed pastry shaped like a small crescent, but to cut down on the fuss, I just make roulades. The Pressburger is made with a yeast-raised short-crust dough (a cross between short-crust pastry and yeast dough. You can't be spontaneous with this delicate pastry: The dough must have its beauty sleep of at least 2 hours in the refrigerator, and the poppy seed mixture must be cold, too (or it will melt the butter in the dough). The result, however, is well worth all the trouble: five insanely fragrant roulades of rich dough and moist poppy seed filling. Strangely enough, even people who don't like poppy seeds as a matter of principle devour these cakes, and the poppy seed enthusiasts will love you forever.

5 ROULADES

FOR THE YEAST STARTER
½ cup (120ml) lukewarm milk

1 tsp sugar

1 tbsp (8g) active dry yeast

FOR THE DOUGH
4 cups (560g) all-purpose flour, plus more for dusting

½ cup (100g) sugar

7 oz (200g) cold butter, diced

2 egg yolks

3½ oz (100ml) sour cream

FOR THE POPPY SEED FILLING
2 cups (480ml) milk

1½ cups (300g) sugar

½ cup (120ml) honey

3½ oz (100g) butter, diced

4 cups (400g) ground poppy seeds

2 egg yolks

Zest of 1 lemon

½ cup (100g) biscuit crumbs

1 cup (240g) apricot jam

FOR THE GLAZE
2 egg yolks, mixed with 1 tsp vinegar

To make the yeast starter, in a cup, combine the milk, sugar and yeast. Set aside for 10 minutes to develop.

To make the dough, in a mixer fitted with the flat attachment, combine the flour, sugar and butter and beat at medium speed for 2 minutes, to a crumbly consistency. Lower the mixer's speed, add the yeast mixture, egg yolks and sour cream, and mix for another minute, until the dough is homogenous, soft and not sticky (no need to knead as much as a regular yeast dough).

Cover the mixer bowl with plastic wrap and transfer to the refrigerator for at least 2 hours (and up to 12 hours). The dough will hardly rise in the refrigerator, and that's okay.

In the meantime, make the poppy seed filling. In a pot over medium heat, bring the milk, sugar, honey and butter to a boil. Reduce the heat to low, mix in the poppy seeds and cook for 15–20 minutes, stirring occasionally, until the mixture thickens. Take off the stove, and let cool to room temperature.

Whisk in the egg yolks, zest and biscuit crumbs and transfer to the refrigerator for an hour to set.

Transfer the cold dough to a floured work surface, and divide into 5 equal parts (work with each part separately and keep the other parts in the refrigerator, so they will not warm and soften up). Roll each part into a roughly 10 x 12-inch (25 x 30.5-cm) thin rectangle. Spread a thin, even layer of apricot jam on the rolled-out dough. Spread a thick layer of the poppy seed filling on the jam layer, and roll into a roulade.

Grease 5 loaf pans. Place the roulades in the pans (they provide support and prevent cracking).

To glaze, brush the egg yolk mixture on the roulades and set aside for 20 minutes (the dough will not rise a lot, and that's okay).

Preheat the oven to 325°F (160°C).

Brush the roulades with the glaze again. To decorate, pass a fork along the surface of the cake in wavy lines (or prick to get dots). Bake for 40 minutes, until browned. Let cool a little before slicing and serving. Keep in the refrigerator.

Gerbeaud—a Hungarian Layered Cake

The layered Hungarian gerbeaud is a favorite of my mom's, and every time I publish a new book, she nags me about including a gerbeaud recipe in it. I had promised twice, and now, finally, I deliver. This cake is baked in a rectangular pan and then cut into squares. It has apricot jam and walnut filling between layers of yeast-raised short-crust dough and a chocolate frosting on top. Mom, this is from me to you, with love.

ONE 13 X 11-INCH (33 X 28-CM) CAKE

FOR THE DOUGH

4 cups (560g) all-purpose flour, plus more for dusting

1 tbsp (8g) active dry yeast

2 tbsp (25g) granulated sugar

Zest of ½ lemon

11 oz (300g) butter or margarine, cold and diced

3 egg yolks (save the whites for the filling)

¾ cup (200ml) sour cream

FOR THE WALNUT FILLING

2 cups (200g) ground walnuts

1 cup (200g) granulated sugar

Zest of ½ lemon

3 egg whites

FOR THE JAM

1 cup (240g) apricot jam

2 tbsp (30ml) boiling water

FOR THE FROSTING

3 tbsp (30g) cocoa powder

1¼ cups (150g) powdered sugar

3 tbsp (45ml) vegetable oil

3 tbsp (45ml) boiling water

To make the dough, in a mixer fitted with the flat attachment, combine the flour, yeast, granulated sugar, lemon zest and butter cubes and beat to a crumbly consistency. Add the egg yolks and sour cream and continue mixing, just until the dough is homogenous and not sticky (no need to knead it as much as a regular yeast dough).

Wrap the dough with plastic wrap, and put in the refrigerator for at least 2 hours (and up to 12 hours). The dough will not rise a lot, and that's okay.

To make the walnut filling, in a bowl, mix together the ground walnuts, granulated sugar and lemon zest.

In a mixer, beat the egg whites at medium speed, until they turn into a soft white froth. Add in the walnut filling, and beat until combined (the meringue will lose volume, and that's okay).

To prepare the jam, combine the jam and boiling water in a small bowl, and mix until it is loose and easy to spread.

Preheat the oven to 350°F (180°C). Grease a 13 x 11-inch (33 x 28-cm) pan with butter or line with parchment paper.

Transfer the cold dough onto a floured work surface, and divide into 3 equal parts (work with each part individually and keep the others in the refrigerator so they won't warm and soften up). Roll out each part to a thin rectangle the size of the pan. Prick one of the parts with a fork to keep it from rising in the oven (this one will go on top).

Place one rectangle in the pan and spread half of the jam on it. Spread half of the walnut filling on the jam, and cover with another dough rectangle. Spread the remaining jam on the dough, then spread the remaining filling on the jam. Put the pricked dough layer on top.

Bake immediately, no need for rising, for 30 minutes, until the cake is golden and risen. Set aside to cool.

Meanwhile, make the frosting. Combine all the frosting ingredients in a bowl and stir to a shiny and thick glaze. Pour it over the cake, and, with the back of a spoon, spread it evenly. Transfer the cake to the refrigerator for at least 2 hours (the texture improves after a couple of hours in the refrigerator). Slice into small squares, and serve.

A Real Viennese Apple Strudel

I was afraid of making a real strudel. The stretching of the dough was terrifying; what if it tears? So I tried it at home, with my private chef holding my hand. Together, we discovered that this dough is very soft and, what's more important, very elastic, so the stretching is easy. Making a real strudel is indeed a skill, but like all skills, it is acquired. Maybe your first won't be perfect, but believe me, a little tearing is no big deal, and the strudel will still be great. These instructions are precise and detailed so anyone can do it, I promise. If you are new at baking, and are not mentally ready, get a store-bought pastry-puff or filo.

AN ENORMOUS STRUDEL (ABOUT 30 INCHES [76CM] LONG!)

FOR THE DOUGH
⅔ cup (160ml) water

2 tbsp (30ml) vegetable oil

¼ tsp salt

1 tsp vinegar

2 cups (280g) all-purpose flour, plus more for dusting

FOR THE CRISPY BREADCRUMBS
3½ tbsp (50g) butter, for frying

1 cup (100g) breadcrumbs

FOR THE APPLE FILLING
7 large Granny Smith apples

Zest of ½ lemon

2 tbsp (30ml) lemon juice

1 cup (200g) granulated sugar

½ tsp ground cinnamon

To make the dough, in a mixer fitted with the kneading attachment, combine the water, oil, salt and vinegar. Add the flour, and mix at medium speed for 10 minutes, until the dough wraps around the kneading attachment and is smooth, shiny, soft and a little sticky.

Grease a length of plastic wrap and wrap the dough in it. Set aside for at least 30 minutes, and up to 2 hours. This is absolutely necessary! If you skip this stage, the dough will tear when you stretch it.

While the dough is resting, prepare the crispy breadcrumbs. In a frying pan, melt the butter. Add the breadcrumbs and fry, stirring constantly, until they become brown and crispy. Remove from the stove and let cool.

To make the filling, peel and core the apples, cut into quarters, cut each quarter into thin slices and put in a bowl. Add the lemon zest and juice, granulated sugar and cinnamon. Set aside for the apples to soak up the flavors while you stretch the dough (the apples will secrete a lot of liquid, and that's okay, just be sure to strain the apples before putting them in the strudel).

Put a clean tablecloth or sheet (nothing made from a fibrous material) on your dining table, and dust generously with flour—really rub it in. Begin by rolling the dough on the tablecloth with a rolling pin. Roll it as thin as you can, flouring as you go (if the dough shrinks back it means that it didn't rest enough—cover it with plastic wrap and let it rest for a few more minutes before resuming the process).

When you have rolled out the dough as much as you can, begin to stretch it with your hands: walk around the table and gently pull out the edges. Walk and stretch, walk and stretch. After 4 or 5 rounds, the dough should be about 40 x 40 inches (100 x 10cm). Remember, a torn and thin dough is better than an intact thick one. If the edges are a little thick, cut them off before filling your strudel.

Preheat the oven to 375°F (190°C). Line a baking sheet with parchment paper.

FOR FINISHING THE STRUDEL

5½ oz (150g) melted butter, lukewarm, divided

Powdered sugar, for dusting

To finish the strudel, pour most of the melted butter on the stretched dough, saving a little for later on. Gently, in patting motions, spread the melted butter with your hands over the stretched dough (a brush might tear it). Sprinkle with the crispy breadcrumbs.

Strain the apples (the liquid in the bowl is not necessary) and lay them across the bottom third of the dough, leaving about 4-inch (10-cm) margins on the bottom and the sides.

Fold the sides of the dough (that are without filling) inward, toward the center, to close the strudel's edges. Using the cloth, fold the lower side of the dough over the filling. Keep rolling with the cloth, until you get a very long (30 inches [76cm]) plump roulade. Carefully transfer the roulade to the prepared baking sheet (lift the strudel on your arm, laying it in the baking tray in a U shape, so it fits in).

Pour most of the remaining melted butter onto the strudel and with your hands, spread it to cover the whole strudel (save some melted butter to glaze the strudel after baking). Put in the oven, and bake for 40 minutes, until browned (the bottom, too).

Take the strudel out of the oven and immediately brush it with the melted butter (if the butter has hardened, melt it again in the microwave oven). Dust with the powdered sugar, slice and serve.

GRANDMA KNOWS BEST

As long as we knead the dough for at least 10 minutes, and let it rest for at least half an hour, it will lend itself to the stretching process with the flexibility of a Pilates instructor. And how much to stretch? Until it is translucent and any more stretching will tear it (if it tears a little, it's okay; better to be a thin and torn dough than an intact thick one). They used to say that the dough must be so thin you should be able to read the newspaper through it. Nowadays, you should be able to search the Internet on your iPhone through it.

AND GRANDPA WOULD SAY

Grandpa Micha (who is also my dad) says that a strudel without vanilla sauce is not a strudel! So, here is a sauce option:

A quick way to prepare the classic sauce: Whisk together 1 cup (240ml) milk, 3 egg yolks, ⅓ cup (70g) sugar, 1 teaspoon cornstarch and ½ teaspoon vanilla extract (or the seeds from ½ vanilla pod), until combined. Put in a pot and cook over medium heat, whisking constantly, just until the mixture thickens a little and steam begins to rise (180°F [82°C] if you have a thermometer; do not boil!). Strain, cover the surface of the sauce with plastic wrap and cool. Keep for up to 2 days in the refrigerator.

Stretch the dough to 40 x 40 inches (100 x 100 cm).

Pour melted butter on the dough.

Layer breadcrumbs and apples on the dough.

WHO STOLE THE COOKIES FROM THE COOKIE JAR?

Any grandmother I have ever known had one of those: a mysterious tin or jar filled with homemade cookies.

Meringue Rose Cookies

The grandmothers keep these cookies in an old tin box under the bed, and rightly so! Displayed in a fancy, see-through glass jar on the kitchen counter, they will not last very long. These cookies are made with yolk-enriched short-crust pastry, and the whites are used for a sweet meringue filling. My personal take on this time-honored recipe is the use of three different pudding flavors: vanilla, dulce de leche and chocolate, but you can make them with one flavor (just mix all the meringue with ½ cup [80g] of the pudding mix of your choice). The biggest challenge here, besides having to decide which flavor to eat first, is the prebaking slicing; you want it to be neat, of course, but it gets squashed a little by the knife. The secret to perfectly sliced cookies is waiting for you in the "Grandma Knows Best" section below.

ABOUT 60 COOKIES

FOR THE DOUGH

2½ cups (350g) all-purpose flour, plus more for dusting

1 tbsp (10g) baking powder

7 oz (200g) cold butter, diced

3 egg yolks (save the whites for the filling)

½ cup (120ml) orange juice or milk

FOR THE MERINGUE

3 egg whites, at room temperature

¾ cup (150g) sugar

2 tbsp (25g) vanilla-flavored instant pudding mix

2 tbsp (25g) dulce de leche–flavored instant pudding mix

2 tbsp (25g) chocolate-flavored instant pudding mix

To make the dough, in a food processor, process the flour, baking powder and butter cubes to a crumbly consistency. Add the egg yolks and orange juice, and mix as little as possible, just until the dough is homogenous. Wrap in plastic wrap, and keep in the refrigerator while preparing the filling.

To make the meringue in three flavors, in a mixer, beat the egg whites at medium speed until they turn into a soft white froth with bubbles (about 30 seconds). Gradually add the sugar one spoonful at a time, with 10-second intervals between spoonfuls. Turn the speed to high, and continue beating for another 3 minutes, until the meringue is smooth, shiny and creamy and all the sugar granules are dissolved.

Divide the meringue equally among 3 bowls. To each bowl, add the pudding mix of one of the flavors, and mix gently to incorporate.

Preheat the oven to 350°F (180°C). Line a baking sheet with parchment paper.

Divide the dough into 3 equal parts. Roll each part on a floured sheet of parchment paper to a thin (less than ¼ inch [6mm]) rectangle of about 8 x 16 inches (20 x 41cm). Spread on each dough rectangle one of the flavored meringues. Roll into a roulade (with the help of the parchment paper under it). Slice each roulade into 1-inch (2.5-cm) slices. For neat and pretty slices, freeze the roulades for about half an hour, until they harden, and then slice (see the "Grandma Knows Best" section below). Lay the slices flat (and spaciously) on the prepared baking sheet.

Bake for about 15 minutes, until the dough is golden and the meringue is dry to the touch (The cookies are supposed to maintain a light color). Cool and keep in a sealed box under the bed . . .

GRANDMA KNOWS BEST

If you insist on slicing the roulades of meringue-filled dough right after rolling, the slices will squash and the filling will ooze out. For a prettier result, freeze the roulades for half an hour, until both dough and filling harden. Slice with a knife dipped in boiling water (wiping it dry between cuts).

Butter Cookies, Just like Grandma's

This is the perfect dough to make with children; it is very easy to roll out, doesn't stick and doesn't require any time in the refrigerator (the Kichlach dough on page 161 is also great for this purpose). The cookies from this dough are simple—and great tasting—"Grandma cookies." I love their buttery flavor (reminiscent of the Danish butter cookies that come in those round blue tins), but these cookies can be made with margarine if you prefer. Choose any size and shape you want; however, it is important that all the cookies in the same baking tray are of the same thickness and size. If they are different, the thinner, smaller cookies will burn before the larger, thicker ones are cooked.

ABOUT 60 COOKIES

3 cups (420g) all-purpose flour, plus more for dusting

1 tsp baking powder

1 cup (200g) sugar, plus more for sprinkling (optional)

7 oz (200g) cold butter, diced

2 eggs

Preheat the oven to 350°F (180°C). Line a baking sheet with parchment paper.

In a food processor, process the flour, baking powder, sugar and butter cubes to a crumbly consistency. Add the eggs and mix just until you get a ball of dough.

Roll the dough out on a floured sheet of parchment paper, cut out cookies with a cup or a cookie cutter of the shape of your choice, and spaciously lay on the prepared baking sheet. You can sprinkle a little sugar on the cookies, if you like.

Bake for 15–20 minutes, depending on the cookies' size and thickness, until golden. Let cool completely and keep in a closed container, at room temperature.

GRANDMA KNOWS BEST

Especially cute cookie cutters (like the ones in the picture) make all the difference between plain cookies and cookies that put a smile on your face every time you pass by the cookie jar. I used some original cookie cutters in shapes that kids like, but any cutter with a pattern will do. Bear in mind that with these cutters, you have to press down hard enough (and not too hard, so as not to perforate and tear the dough) for the pattern to show after baking. Experiment and experience are key; after a few cookies, you will know.

Creamookies—Vanilla Cookies Filled with Nutella Cream

Like their Israeli name (*kremugit*), Creamookies are a combination of cream and cookie. As a teenager, I had a secret nocturnal habit (at least I thought it was secret; mom knew all along . . .): I loved reading under my down comforter with a flashlight, long after my bedtime. Reading made me hungry, so, for practical reasons—they melt in your mouth and make no crunching noise—*kremugit* were my midnight snack of choice. So, you see, these cookies are nostalgic to me. To celebrate the 100,000 "likes" on my Facebook page, I shared a recipe for these vanilla cookies with their oozy chocolate filling, and the response was so favorable that I just had to include it in this book. Prepare and eat these straight out of the oven, when they are still warm. If the cookies cool down, you can heat them in the microwave oven so the Nutella filling will soften. If you are the dip-the-cookie-in-coffee type, you are in for a treat.

25 COOKIES

1 cup (320g) Nutella

5½ oz (150g) butter, softened

1 cup (200g) sugar

1 tsp vanilla extract

1 egg

2 cups (280g) all-purpose flour

½ tsp baking soda

½ tsp salt

GRANDMA KNOWS BEST

Before you ask—yes, of course you can substitute the Nutella with any other paste you like: chocolate, walnuts, dulce de leche, lotus seed, halva—you name it. The principle is the same; use a fatty paste (fruit jams and marmalades will not do).

Prepare the frozen Nutella "coins" (instructions below).

Preheat the oven to 350°F (180°C). Line a baking sheet with parchment paper.

In a mixer fitted with the flat attachment, beat the butter, sugar and vanilla to a creamy consistency. Add the egg and mix until combined.

Add the flour, baking soda and salt, and mix until the dough is homogenous and soft.

Make 25 little dough balls, and flatten them down like pita bread. Place a frozen Nutella coin in the center of each "pita," close and reshape as a ball. Place the balls spaciously on the prepared baking sheet.

Bake for 10 minutes, until the cookies flatten a little and their edges turn gold (they should remain light in color). Let cool a little, and devour. Keep in a closed container at room temperature (to serve, heat each cookie in the microwave oven for 15 seconds to soften the Nutella filling).

HOW COME NOBODY THOUGHT OF THIS BEFORE?!

For easy filling of the Creamookies, prepare and freeze Nutella "coins." Line a baking sheet with parchment paper and spoon little mounds of Nutella onto the paper. You can do it with two teaspoons, with a small piping bag or with a sandwich bag that you cut off one of its corners. Freeze them until they are hard (1 hour). If the Nutella coins soften during preparation, return them to the freezer for a few minutes before resuming.

Super Great Chocolate Chip Cookies

Good recipes for chocolate chip cookies are a dime a dozen, and after the many options in my previous books, I was reluctant to include yet another one here; however, this recipe is really special. The reason for the wonderful texture is the baking powder in this recipe, in addition to the baking soda. The beautiful golden color is achieved by a perfect white to brown sugar ratio, but the wildest upgrade here is the filling—Nutella or any other chocolate spread—hiding in the cookies (added in the same easy—and fun—manner explained in the Creamookies recipe on page 128).

30 LARGE COOKIES

1 cup (320g) Nutella

7 oz (200g) butter, softened

1 cup (200g) granulated sugar

¾ cup (180g) packed dark brown sugar

2 tsp (10ml) vanilla extract

2 eggs

2¾ cups (390g) all-purpose flour

2 tsp (8g) baking powder

1 tsp baking soda

½ tsp salt

2 cups (300g) chocolate chips

Prepare the frozen Nutella "coins" as explained on page 128.

Preheat the oven to 350°F (180°C). Line a baking sheet with parchment paper.

In a mixer fitted with the flat attachment, beat the butter, both sugars and vanilla for 2 minutes at medium speed, until creamy. The brown sugar will not dissolve, and that's okay.

Add the eggs, one at a time, and mix until combined (add the next egg only after the previous one is completely incorporated). Add the flour, baking powder, baking soda and salt, and mix until a soft dough is formed. Add the chocolate chips (you may want to save about a handful for garnish), and mix only until they are distributed in the dough.

With wet hands, make dough balls (the size of ping-pong balls). You can also use an ice cream scoop for this purpose. Flatten the balls to the shape of a small "pita." Place a frozen Nutella coin in the center of each "pita," close and roll into a ball again. At this point, if you want your cookies to be as gorgeous as the ones in the picture, stick a few chocolate chips in each one as garnish.

Spaciously arrange the dough balls on the prepared baking sheet. Bake for about 15 minutes, until the cookies have flattened a little, are brown and firm around the edges and still light and soft in the center (they will set during cooling). Let cool a little, and serve (they are best eaten warm). Keep in a closed container at room temperature. When served later, I recommend that you heat them in a microwave oven for 15 seconds, to soften the Nutella filling.

GRANDMA KNOWS BEST

If you want to serve the cookies as demonstrated here, after baking, use a thick skewer or a small piping tip to make a hole on the side of each cookie. Place each cookie over the rim of a glass filled with cold milk, and insert a colorful drinking straw through the hole.

AND ANOTHER THING

Be warned that after you take your first bite of a Nutella-filled chocolate chip cookie, regular chocolate chip cookies will never taste as good as they used to. This is how they look on the inside—yummm.

Black and White Cookies

What are you in the mood for? Spiral cookies? Teddy bear cookies? Target cookies or free-for-all cookies? Or maybe you are in a checkerboard frame of mind? These are all black and white cookies that begin as separate chocolate and vanilla doughs (that take seconds in the food processor). In my upgraded version, the brown dough contains dark chocolate as well as cocoa powder. The final product is the result of some design games. It may look sophisticated, but it is actually very easy (go to pages 90–91 for the precise instructions). This recipe yields a large amount of cookies, but I think that if you take the trouble to prepare two kinds of dough, you might as well have something to show for it (and you can always freeze some of them). Make sure you use cold eggs in this recipe—this will enable you to roll it out straight away, without having to wait until it has "rested" in the refrigerator.

ABOUT 60 COOKIES

FOR THE VANILLA DOUGH

3 cups (420g) all-purpose flour

½ tsp baking powder

1 cup (200g) sugar

7 oz (200g) cold butter, diced

2 eggs, cold from the refrigerator

2 tsp (10ml) vanilla extract

FOR THE CHOCOLATE DOUGH

3½ oz (100g) dark chocolate

3 cups (420g) all-purpose flour

½ tsp baking powder

¼ cup (40g) cocoa powder

1¼ cups (250g) sugar

7 oz (200g) cold butter, diced

2 eggs, cold from the refrigerator

Begin with the vanilla dough (so there is no need to clean the food processor bowl). In a food processor, process the flour, baking powder, sugar and butter cubes to a crumbly consistency. Add the eggs and vanilla, and mix just until a ball of dough forms. If the dough is dry and breaks into crumbs, add 1 tablespoon (15ml) cold water, and if it is too sticky add 1 tablespoon (8g) flour. Set aside (in the summer, put in the refrigerator.)

To make the chocolate dough, in a microwave-safe bowl, melt the chocolate in a microwave oven and set aside for 5 minutes to cool.

In the food processor (no need to clean), process the flour, baking powder, cocoa powder, sugar and butter cubes to a crumbly consistency. Add the eggs and mix a little. Add the melted chocolate and mix just until a ball of dough forms. If the dough is dry and breaks into crumbs, add 1 tablespoon (15ml) cold water. If it is too sticky, add 1 tablespoon (8g) flour. Shape the cookies as desired (see pages 134–135).

Preheat the oven to 350°F (180°C). Line a few baking sheets with parchment paper.

Bake for 15–20 minutes, until the vanilla dough is golden. Let cool and keep in a closed container at room temperature.

GRANDMA KNOWS BEST

The grandmothers used to make one dough, divide it in half and knead cocoa powder into one of the halves. I prefer to prepare two separate doughs, to avoid over-kneading (not good for the crispiness of the cookies). Thanks to this separation, melted chocolate can be added to upgrade the brown dough.

AND ANOTHER THING

It is very important to measure the amount of baking powder; too much of it will cause the cookies to lose their shape during baking.

Teddy Bear Cookies

On 2 lightly floured parchment sheets, roll out each of the doughs to ¼-inch (6-mm) thick. Cut out the same number of big circles from each dough; cut twice as many (2 to 1) small circles from each dough. Place a big circle (the "head") on a paper-lined baking tray. Brush a small circle of the opposite color with a little water, and stick it on the big circle, a little below its center—that's the "nose." Cut another small circle (the same color as the "nose") in half, brush the cut on each half with water, and stick them to the big circle's circumference to make the teddy bear's "ears." After baking, use a little chocolate spread to stick small M&Ms over the nose to create the "eyes."

Target Cookies

On 2 lightly floured parchment sheets, roll out each of the doughs to ¼-inch (6-mm) thick. Prepare circular cookie cutters of three sizes—large, medium and small.

Cut the same number of large circles out of both doughs and place them spaciously on a paper-lined baking tray. Cut a medium and a small circle out of each cookie. Now each cookie is made of three circles—large, medium and small. Carefully remove the middle (medium) circle out of each cookie and replace it with one of the opposite color. Repeat with all the cookies. Sprinkle with a little sugar for garnish.

Free-for-All Cookies

Gather all the edges and extra dough from the preparation of all the other designs, knead them together and roll into a long cylinder. Cut into slices just under ½-inch (1.3-cm) thick.

Zebra Cookies

On 2 lightly floured parchment sheets, roll out each of the doughs to a ¼-inch (6-mm) thick rectangle. Cut each rectangle into 3 equal rectangles, and remove any excess flour with a dry brush. Brush each rectangle with water and place them on top of each other, alternating colors. Wrap in plastic wrap and freeze for 20 minutes to harden. Slice into ¼-inch (6-mm) thick slices.

Checkerboard Cookies

Follow the instructions for Zebra Cookies up to the wrapping and freezing. Slice into strips just under ½-inch (1.3-cm) thick. Brush a strip with water and place another one on it, making sure that the black strips are on the white ones and vice versa. Now brush the cookie on top with water and place another one on it in the same manner.

Freeze for 20 minutes to harden, and cut into ¼-inch (6-mm) thick squares.

Spiral Cookies

On 2 lightly floured parchment sheets, roll out each of the doughs to a ¼-inch (6-mm) thick rectangle. With a knife, trim the edges of the dough rectangles to make them straight and even. With a dry brush, remove any excess flour. Brush the chocolate dough with a little water and place the vanilla rectangle on it. Roll them together into a roulade. Wrap in plastic wrap, and put in the freezer for 20 minutes to harden.

Sprinkle sugar on a baking tray. Brush the roulade with a little water and roll in the sugar to coat. Cut into ¼-inch (6mm) thick slices.

Soft and Plump Cinnamon Cookies

The word "awesome!" was scribbled in mom's old recipe notebook next to this recipe. Moms are always right, as you well know. It is also true that sometimes all we need are simple comfort cookies with our coffee, like these gigantic, softer than soft (with a little crunch around the edges) cinnamon cookies. Most of all, they remind me of muffin tops. I like making them because they are delicious of course, but also because of the cinnamon and butter aroma that fills the house when they are in the oven.

25 LARGE COOKIES

7 oz (200g) butter, softened

1½ cups (300g) sugar

2 tsp (10ml) vanilla extract

2 eggs

3 cups (420g) all-purpose flour

2 tsp (8g) baking powder

½ tsp salt

2 tsp (4g) ground cinnamon

¼ cup (60ml) milk

FOR COATING

¼ cup (50g) sugar + 1 tbsp (6g) ground cinnamon, mixed together

Preheat the oven to 350°F (180°C). Line a baking sheet with parchment paper.

In a mixer fitted with the flat attachment, mix the butter and sugar to a creamy consistency. Add the vanilla and eggs (one at a time), and mix until combined. Add the flour, baking powder, salt, cinnamon and milk, and mix until combined. The dough will be soft and a little sticky.

With wet hands or an ice cream scoop, shape into balls (ping-pong ball size). To coat, roll them in the sugar and cinnamon mixture. Spaciously arrange the balls on the prepared baking sheet.

Bake for only 10–12 minutes; it is very important not to overbake, or the cookies will be too dry. They are ready when they are puffed up, with firm edges and a very soft center. Let cool a little (when cooled, the edges become crispier, but the cookies will remain soft and moist in the middle).

GRANDMA KNOWS BEST

I don't like to be caught unprepared, so I always have some cinnamon dough balls (without the cinnamon and sugar coating) in my freezer. I make them, arrange them on a tray (as if I am getting ready to bake them), and put the tray in the freezer. After 2–3 hours, when the dough balls are rock hard, I put them in a plastic bag (they are frozen solid, so they won't stick). They will keep like this for up to 2 months. When you want to bake them, take out the amount you need, place the balls on a paper-lined baking sheet and let sit until they are partially defrosted and begin to "sweat" a little so the sugar and cinnamon coating will stick to them. Roll in the coating, and bake. I have been known to bake only four cookies for my private chef and I, to go with our morning coffee; this way we are not tempted to gobble down the whole jar later on in the day.

Addictive Sandwich Cookies

Everyone knows the basic, old-time short-crust pastry—the "1-2-3 dough" (100g sugar, 200g margarine, 300g flour, and an egg). Here, for your pleasure, is my "100-200-2-2" (in Hebrew it sounds like a nursery rhyme, and the numbers help me remember the recipe) upgrade—100g powdered sugar, 200g butter, 2 cups (280 g) flour, 2 egg yolks. That's all you need—no baking powder, no liquids, no salt and not even vanilla extract. This is a perfect dough. Besides cookies, they also make gorgeous, melt-in-your-mouth hamantaschen (the Purim triangular pastry, see page 179). To me, however, the best thing to do with this dough is to make sandwich cookies of all shapes and fillings: Nutella hearts, jam circles, dulce de leche flowers, halva triangles (and I can go on and on . . .). They are all pretty and all very tasty. They are crispy on the day of baking, and soft the day after, but either way, they are addictive.

30 SANDWICH COOKIES

¾ cup (100g) powdered sugar

7 oz (200g) cold butter, diced

2 cups (280g) all-purpose flour, plus more for dusting

2 egg yolks

Jam or any other paste you like—about 1 cup (240g)

Powdered sugar

In a food processor, process the powdered sugar, butter cubes and flour to a crumbly consistency. Add the egg yolks and mix as little as possible, just until a ball of dough forms. If the dough is too dry, add 1 tablespoon (15ml) milk. If it is too sticky, add 1 tablespoon (8g) flour. Wrap with plastic wrap, and put in the refrigerator for 2 hours to set.

Preheat the oven to 325°F (160°C). Line a few baking sheets with parchment paper.

Roll the cold dough out on a floured sheet of parchment paper, until just under ¼-inch (6-mm) thick. Cut out the shape or shapes of your choice (stars, flowers, hearts, etc.), and place on the prepared baking sheets (see the "Grandma Knows Best" section below). In the centers of half of the cookies, cut out a little circle (or any other shape). Roll out any excess dough and repeat.

Bake for 15 minutes, until slightly golden. Let cool completely.

Place a generous teaspoon of the filling of your choice on the cookies without the holes. Generously dust the cookies with holes with the powdered sugar. Carefully place the top cookies (with the holes) on the bottom ones, and press ever so lightly. Keep in a closed container, in a single layer, at room temperature.

AND ANOTHER THING

If you are stuck without egg yolks, put in 2–3 tablespoons (30–45ml) milk instead. The dough will be less flaky and melt-in-your-mouth, but it will still be very tasty.

AND GRANDMA WOULD SAY

You can prepare double the amount of dough, bake twice as many cookies, and freeze some (or all) of them: wrap the cookies you want to freeze (without filling or powdered sugar). They will keep in the freezer for up to a month. When you want to serve the cookies, defrost for 1 hour on the counter, and sandwich them.

GRANDMA KNOWS BEST

It is better to bake the cookies with the holes on a separate tray, because they take less time to bake. Also, note the relative low baking temperature—the cookies must be light gold. Do not let them brown, or they will lose their perfect texture.

Jam and Crumb Squares

One look at these nostalgic cookies, with the jam showing through the crumbs, and you know that they will taste like home (and like more . . .). And I haven't even mentioned how easy they are to make: You make the dough in the food processor (takes seconds), spread part of it as the base and grate the rest for the coating. You bake the whole thing in a large baking tray, and after baking, you cut it into squares.

THIRTY-FIVE 2-INCH (5-CM) SQUARES

2 cups (280g) all-purpose flour

1 cup (100g) ground almonds

½ cup (100g) sugar

7 oz (200g) cold butter, diced

2 egg yolks

1½ cups (360g) jam

Preheat the oven to 350°F (180°C). Line a 13 x 11-inch (33 x 28-cm) baking pan with parchment paper.

In a food processor, process the flour, almonds, sugar and butter cubes to a crumbly consistency. Add the egg yolks and mix in short pulses, just until the dough is homogenous. Wrap one-third of the dough in plastic wrap and put in the freezer for 20 minutes to harden a little.

In the meantime, press the rest of the dough into the bottom and sides (up to ½ inch [1.3cm]) of the prepared pan (see the "Grandma Knows Best" section below) and bake for 15 minutes, until golden.

Take out of the oven, leaving it on, and carefully spread the jam over the baked base. If the jam is too thick, you can add a little boiling water to soften it. Take out the reserved dough that you put in the freezer, and grate it through the large holes of a grater over the jam, until covered.

Return to the oven and bake for another 20 minutes, until golden. Let cool, and cut into squares. Keep in a closed container at room temperature.

AND ANOTHER THING

Don't forego the ground almonds—they make the dough more delicate and add to the flavor as well. If you want these cookies to be harder and crunchier, substitute the egg yolks with one whole egg.

GRANDMA KNOWS BEST

It is important to line the bottom and about ½ inch (1.3cm) of the sides of the pan with the dough—this makes it easier to extract it from the pan after baking (when cooled, the jam hardens and might stick to the sides).

Jam and Coconut-Meringue Cutouts

I made these cookies for the first time when I was in my teens. It was in my mom's recipe book marked "great!" Everybody loved it, but it took me many years to brave the kitchen again. At age 26 (and change), when I discovered—and fell in love with—baking, one of my first ventures was to confiscate mom's old and tattered books (replacing them with new copies), and prepare each and every recipe sporting a complimentary footnote. Over the years, I have gained experience and confidence and started to develop my own recipes. Returning to this one, I updated and upgraded it a little: butter instead of margarine, egg yolks instead of whole eggs and some other touch-ups. Make it, and savor the dreamy, melt-in-your-mouth little bites of short-crust pastry, jam and coconut meringue.

THIRTY-FIVE 2-INCH (5-CM) SQUARES

FOR THE BASE
2 cups (280g) all-purpose flour

2 tsp (6g) baking powder

½ cup (100g) sugar

7 oz (200g) cold butter, diced

4 egg yolks (save the whites for the coconut meringue)

FOR THE JAM LAYER
1 cup (240g) strawberry jam

FOR THE COCONUT MERINGUE
4 egg whites

¾ cup (150g) sugar

1 cup (100g) desiccated coconut

2 tbsp (20g) vanilla-flavored instant pudding mix

To make the base, preheat the oven to 350°F (180°C). Line a 13 x 11-inch (33 x 28-cm) baking pan with parchment paper.

In a food processor, process the flour, baking powder, sugar and butter cubes to a crumbly consistency. Add the egg yolks and mix just until you get a ball of dough.

With your hands, press the dough into the prepared pan and bake for 20 minutes, until golden. Take out of the oven, and leave it on. Let cool a little.

To make the jam layer, in a microwave oven, heat the jam for 20 seconds, until runny and smooth. Spread it over the baked base, and set aside.

To make the meringue, in a mixer, beat the egg whites at medium speed, until they turn into a soft white froth full of bubbles (about 30 seconds). Gradually add the sugar, and beat until the meringue is firm and shiny. Lower the mixer's speed to minimum, add the desiccated coconut and pudding mix, and beat for 5 more seconds, just until incorporated (the meringue will lose some of its volume, and that's okay).

Spread the meringue over the jam layer; return the pan to the oven and bake for 20–25 minutes, until golden.

Let cool completely, cut into squares (or triangles) and keep covered in the refrigerator. After a few hours, the cookies become very soft—really worth the wait.

GRANDMA KNOWS BEST
Initially crispy and crunchy, the texture of these cookies improves significantly on the next day. The time in the refrigerator causes the dough and the meringue to become mushy and soft like a cloud.

Nostalgic Date Roulades

Every grandmother makes these roulades, and that is why there are so many versions of them. This one (or something like it) can be found in any self-respecting Moroccan household. The dough calls for margarine as well as oil. The texture is similar to ma'amouls (page 145): sandy at first, then they melt in your mouth. Yummm. I like to drizzle a little raw tahini and sprinkle sesame seeds over the dates for a halva-like "undertone."

5 ROULADES (ABOUT 80 COOKIES)

FOR THE DOUGH
6 cups (840g) all-purpose flour

1 tbsp (10g) baking powder

7 oz (200g) margarine or butter, softened

1 cup (240ml) vegetable oil

1 cup (240ml) water

FOR THE DATE FILLING
2 lb (900g) date paste

2 tsp (4g) ground cinnamon

¼ tsp ground cloves

2 cups (200g) chopped walnuts

FOR HALVA FLAVOR (OPTIONAL)
¾ cup (180g) raw tahini

¼ cup (36g) sesame seeds

Preheat the oven to 350°F (180°C). Line a few baking sheets with parchment paper.

To make the dough, in a mixer fitted with the flat attachment, mix the flour, baking powder, margarine and oil at medium speed to a crumbly consistency. Add the water, and mix until the dough is smooth, soft and not sticky (if it is sticky, add a little flour, and if it is dry, add a little water).

To make the filling, mix the date paste with the cinnamon and cloves, and set aside.

Divide the dough into 5 equal parts. Roll each part out on a floured sheet of parchment paper to a 10 x 12-inch (25 x 30.5-cm) rectangle, about ⅛-inch (3-mm) thick. Spread a thin, even layer of the seasoned date paste on each dough rectangle. Sprinkle the chopped walnuts and—if you want the halva flavor—drizzle with the raw tahini and sprinkle with the sesame seeds. With the help of the parchment paper under the dough, roll into a roulade.

Put the roulades spaciously on the prepared baking sheets. Slice into 1¼-inch (3-cm) slices—make sure you don't cut all the way through (the slices should remain attached at the base). To make slicing easier, you can put the unbaked roulades in the freezer for a few minutes (see the "Grandma Knows Best" section below).

Bake for about 30 minutes, until golden (the cookies are supposed to remain quite light in color). Let cool completely, and cut into individual cookies following the slicing marks. Keep in a closed container at room temperature.

GRANDMA KNOWS BEST
Because slicing is done before baking, I like to freeze the roulades for 20 minutes first, for a sharp and elegant result.

Kourabiedes—Greek Butter Cookies

These are the most melt-in-your-mouth cookies I know. I got the recipe from Ms. Yael Kalderon, who is not only drop-dead gorgeous (with mesmerizing feline eyes) but also an extremely gifted pastry chef. Greek by birth, Yael learned this recipe from her Yaya, who also taught her how to "perfume" the cookies by filling your palms with rose water and dripping it over the cookies as soon as they are taken out of the oven. Yael says that the baking must be short, so the cookies will be light gold, and she is right; if they brown up, they don't melt in your mouth and lose a lot of their charm.

45 COOKIES

2 cups (280g) all-purpose flour

2 tbsp (20g) powdered sugar, plus more for dusting

7 oz (200g) cold butter, diced

2 tbsp (30ml) brandy

¼ cup (60ml) rose water (not essence)

Preheat the oven to 325°F (160°C). Line a few baking sheets with parchment paper.

In a food processor, process the flour, powdered sugar and butter cubes to a crumbly consistency. Add the brandy, and mix just until the dough is homogenous, velvety to the touch and not sticky. If the dough is dry and crumbling, add 1 tablespoon (15ml) brandy. If it is too sticky, add 1 tablespoon (8g) flour.

Roll chunks of dough into 5-inch (12.5-cm) long and ⅔-inch (8-mm) thick cylinders. Close each cylinder to form a ring, and stick the ends together. Place on the prepared baking sheets.

Bake for 15–20 minutes, until the cookies puff up and just start to get a little golden on their bottom side (the color on top will remain unchanged).

Take out of the oven. Pour some rose water into the palm of your hand, and drip it over the hot cookies in the pan (you don't have to do it one cookie at a time, just drip rose water over the whole pan; the perfume will "travel" on its own). Generously dust with powdered sugar. Keep in a sealed container at room temperature.

GRANDMA KNOWS BEST

Did you know you can make your own powdered sugar? All you need is a spice grinder (the food processor doesn't grind finely enough). You must clean the grinder thoroughly to remove any spice smells. To do this, grind 2 tablespoons (30 g) of regular sugar and a teaspoon of baking soda (the sugar granules will clean any residual spices and the baking soda will neutralize the smell. Don't wash the grinder—it will be ruined!). After the sugar and soda cleaning, empty the grinder, and wipe it with a paper towel (watch your fingers!). Grind the sugar (in small batches) to a fine powder. Sift the powder through a fine sifter (you can grind again any granules that did not pass through the sifter). Use immediately, or if you want to use it later, add a little potato starch or cornstarch (2 teaspoons [6g] to 1 cup [140g] powdered sugar) to prevent crystallization. Store in a sealed container.

Ghriba—Moroccan Sand Cookies

Most sweets of Moroccan origin are not very "subtle"; they are deep-fried, drenched in syrup and covered with sesames and sprinkles. Ghriba, on the other hand, are very delicate. They are crumbly, melt-in-your-mouth white balls, with a buttery taste (though you can make them with margarine). These cookies are not too sweet; they are soft and delicate, with a hint of rose water in their flavor (some powdered sugar on them would boost the sweetness a little, if a boost is needed—taste first).

70–80 BITE-SIZE COOKIES

3½ cups (500g) all-purpose flour

1 tsp baking powder

¾ cup (100g) powdered sugar

7 oz (200g) cold butter, diced

⅔ cup (160ml) vegetable oil

1 tbsp (15ml) rose water (not essence)

Peeled pistachio nuts (or halved almonds), unroasted, for garnish

Preheat the oven to 325°F (160°C). Line a few baking sheets with parchment paper.

In a food processor, process the flour, baking powder, powdered sugar and butter cubes to a crumbly consistency. Add the oil and rose water, and mix for a few more seconds, to get a homogenous and velvety ball of dough (roll a little ball of dough to check whether it is too dry or too sticky. Add a spoonful of oil or a spoonful of flour, respectively).

Form little balls of dough (about the size of a cherry tomato). Spaciously lay them on the prepared baking sheets. Gently press a pistachio or half an almond into the center of each ball as garnish.

Bake for about 10 minutes, until the cookies begin to crack and are dry inside (open one to check). The cookies are supposed to be light in color and soft (they will set during cooling). Let cool completely before serving. Keep in a closed container at room temperature.

GRANDMA KNOWS BEST

Make sure you press the pistachio nuts firmly into the dough balls, so they don't fall off during baking, which would leave the cookies with a strange indentation on top, and a little less pretty. In our family, it is also crucial to keep them as far away as possible from my sister Dana, who loves to pick the pistachio or almonds off the cookies and eat them all, no matter how deep I stick them in.

Moroccan Machine Cookies

Most of my time in the kitchen is dedicated to developing new recipes: invent-try-taste-change-try-taste, and so on and so forth. A successful new recipe is always a love story, but I love old recipes just as much. These machine cookies have been with me for many years now. I prepare them again and again; they have their own jar on the counter, and another container in the freezer. The dough is easy to make and easy to work with, even though there are no eggs in this recipe. Unlike most recipes in this book, I must insist on margarine here—this is one of those grandmother recipes you just don't mess with!

ABOUT 80 LARGE COOKIES

6 cups (850g) all-purpose flour

2 heaping tbsp (20g) baking powder

7 oz (200g) melted margarine

1 cup (240ml) vegetable oil

1¼ cups (250g) sugar

1 tsp vanilla extract

1 cup (240ml) orange juice

½ cup (80g) sesame seeds

½ cup (50g) desiccated coconut

Put all the ingredients in a large bowl and knead with your hands for 1 minute, just until the dough is homogenous. Set aside for 10 minutes.

In the meantime, preheat the oven to 325°F (160°C) and assemble a grinder with the special cookie attachment (see the "Grandma Knows Best" section below). Line a few baking sheets with parchment paper.

Pass the dough through the machine (pack it in like you would with meat). With your hands, cut the ribbon that comes out of the machine every 4 inches (10cm) or so. Lay the "fingers" of dough on the prepared baking sheets.

Bake for 25 minutes, until golden. Let cool completely, and keep in a closed container at room temperature.

GRANDMA KNOWS BEST

To get the unique shape and the melt-in-your-mouth texture, you must have a meat grinder and the special cookie attachment (which you can get at any housewares store). I keep a separate grinder for these cookies (while the private chef, who needs his meat minced, uses the grinding attachment on the mixer). See the little step-by-step pictures for smooth and easy assembly. Note that the grinding knife part is not used for these cookies.

Fit the round part of the cookie attachment onto the meat grinder disc (the one with the largest holes).

Secure the locking ring.

Slide the metal bar and choose desired shape.

Sweet Fluffy Bagels (Ka'aks)

Remember the movie *Honey, I Shrunk the Kids?* Well, this recipe is definitely a take on the sequel, *Honey, I Blew Up the Cookies*. They rise a lot (a whole lot!); they almost triple their size in the oven, so make sure you pipe them relatively thin, and leave enough space between them on the baking sheet. These simple cookies are reminiscent of "cat tongues," and I like them best in the winter to dip in my coffee or tea. In our family, the little ones also love them. You should see my baby niece, Shelly, nibbling on them with her two little teeth—what a sweetheart!

ABOUT 5O COOKIES

4 eggs, at room temperature

1 cup (200g) sugar

¾ cup (180ml) vegetable oil

1 tsp vanilla extract

Zest of ½ lemon or orange

3 cups (420g) all-purpose flour

1 tbsp (10g) baking powder

Preheat the oven to 350°F (180°C). Line a few baking sheets with parchment paper.

In a mixer, beat the eggs and sugar at high speed for 10 minutes, to get a light, thick, mousse-like batter.

Lower the mixer's speed to minimum, and slowly drizzle in the oil. Add the vanilla, lemon zest, flour and baking powder, and beat slowly, until the dough is smooth, soft and very sticky.

Transfer the dough to a piping bag with either a serrated or a smooth tip that is not too wide (less than ½ inch [1.3cm]). Pipe rings approximately 2½ inches (6.4cm) wide onto the prepared baking sheets. Make sure the rings are spaced out, because they triple in size in the oven. Piping will require a little "elbow grease."

Bake for 15 minutes, until the cookies rise and are golden; don't let them get brown. Let cool, and keep in a closed container on the counter.

GRANDMA KNOWS BEST

At high speed, your mixer might "dance" on the counter, skip forward and even fall off (and don't ask how I know that . . .), so don't leave it unsupervised. While you do (making sure no one is watching), how about doing a little dance of your own?

Salty Sesame Bagels

True, this book is all about sweets, but I couldn't resist this magnificent recipe of super-crunchy, sesame-coated salty rings. The dough itself takes no time at all, but then the more time-consuming, patience-requiring work begins. The dough must be rolled into rings, and the rings must be dipped—one at a time—in egg and then in sesame seeds. Sounds a little masochistic, but I find it relaxing and even therapeutic. Sometimes, I even make a double amount, because these cookies can keep for up to a month in a sealed container. I shoo everyone out of the kitchen, and roll and dip, roll and dip for hours—beats going to the shrink, I tell you . . .

150 BAGELS

3½ cups (500g) all-purpose flour

1 tbsp (10g) baking powder

1 tbsp (18g) salt

7 oz (200g) margarine, softened

¼ cup (60ml) vegetable oil

½ cup (120ml) water

1 egg

1 tbsp (15ml) water

1½ cups (210g) sesame seeds

Preheat the oven to 325°F (160°C). Line a few baking sheets with parchment paper.

In a mixer fitted with the flat attachment, mix the flour, baking powder, salt, margarine and oil to a crumbly consistency. Add the water, and mix just until the dough is homogenous and not sticky. If the dough is too dry, add a little water. If it is too sticky, add a little flour.

Roll "snakes" about 5 inches (12.5cm) long and ½-inch (1.3-cm) thick, and close them into rings.

In a bowl, whisk together the egg and water. Place the sesame seeds in another bowl. Dip one side of the ring into the egg wash and immediately dip the same side into the sesame seeds (it helps to use one hand for the egg and the other hand for the seeds). Place the rings on the prepared baking sheet, sesame side up.

Bake for 25 minutes, until the bagels are brown, dry and firm to the touch (they will harden completely when cooled). Let cool before serving. Keep in a closed container on the counter.

GRANDMA KNOWS BEST

Not sure if the cookies are dry and cooked inside? Take one out of the oven and put it in the freezer for instant cooling. After a minute, you can taste it to determine whether its sisters are ready.

Piped Cookies (Using a "Cookie Gun")

These cookies are shaped with a contraption called a "cookie gun." The cookie gun comes with a selection of disks, each of which creates a differently shaped cookie. When I make this recipe, I like to use four or five disks and garnish each shape differently: dipped in melted chocolate, garnished with jam, dusted with powdered sugar or just plain. This gives the impression that I have prepared many kinds of very intricate cookies, while I really made just one batch of dough.

ABOUT 30 COOKIES

7 oz (200g) butter, softened

½ cup (100g) sugar

1 tsp vanilla extract

2 egg yolks

2 cups (280g) all-purpose flour

Preheat the oven to 350°F (180°C). Generously butter a few baking sheets.

In a mixer fitted with the flat attachment, beat the butter, sugar and vanilla at medium speed for 5 minutes (no less, mind you), until the batter is airy and fluffy. Add the egg yolks, and mix for another minute.

Stop and scrape down the sides of the mixer bowl. Add the flour, turn the mixer on to minimum speed and mix just until incorporated. The dough should be nice and soft to the touch, but not sticky. If the dough is too dry, add 1 tablespoon (15ml) water. If it is too sticky, add 1 tablespoon (8g) flour.

Pack the dough into the cookie gun, and attach the desired disk. Spaciously pipe the cookies onto the prepared baking sheets (see the "Grandma Knows Best" section below). Feel free to change disks at any time to get different shapes.

Bake for 10 minutes, until golden. Let cool for a few seconds and, with an angled (or a regular) spatula, release the cookies from the baking sheet. Keep in a closed container at room temperature.

GRANDMA KNOWS BEST

Cookie guns are not complicated, but a little practice won't hurt. The secret to neat results is a clean and dry baking sheet, generously coated with butter or margarine (no parchment paper!). The first two cookies always fail, so don't worry. Clean the bottom of the cookie gun, and pipe on; the rest of them will be gorgeous.

Pack the dough into the cookie gun, and attach the desired disk.

Spaciously pipe the cookies onto a greased baking sheet.

Kichlach—Polish Tea Biscuits

Simple-simple, and crunchy-crunchy cookies. The dough is made by hand (no mixer or food processor), and rolled out immediately (and it is nice and soft, not sticky). My suggestion: Prepare this recipe once a week with the children, put in a large jar, and you will never again be stuck without "something sweet" in the house.

ABOUT 60 COOKIES

4 eggs

¾ cup (150g) sugar, plus more for sprinkling

1 tsp vanilla extract

¾ cup (180ml) vegetable oil

4 cups (560g) all-purpose flour, plus more for dusting

1 tbsp (10g) baking powder

Preheat the oven to 350°F (180°C). Line a few baking sheets with parchment paper.

In a large bowl, vigorously whisk together the eggs, sugar, vanilla and oil for 1 minute, until the batter is light and airy. Add the flour and baking powder and mix with a rubber spatula, just until the dough is yellow, homogenous, soft and not sticky.

Roll the dough out on a floured sheet of parchment paper until it is just less than ¼-inch (6-mm) thick. With a cup (or any shape of cookie cutter), cut out cookies and spaciously arrange on the prepared baking sheets. Sprinkle a little sugar on each cookie.

Bake for about 15 minutes, until the cookies are golden. Let cool and keep in a closed container at room temperature.

GRANDMA KNOWS BEST

These cookies are not very sweet, so don't skip the sprinkle of sugar before baking. If you like, you can mix the sugar with a little cinnamon.

Nicole's Almond Cookies

This is the first recipe I ever published. It was in my first baking article, toward the end of 2000. These are also the first cookies that my sister and I prepared with our mother when we were children. I was assigned the job of pressing the fork around the edges of each cookie, and my little sister was told to press her tiny thumb in the center of each cookie. Originally made with margarine, this recipe is inspired by the great Ruth Sirkis. I like it better with butter (sorry, Mom). Since I first published this recipe, I have upgraded it even more; now I make it with powdered sugar instead of granulated sugar—the cookies are even more melt-in-your-mouth. To this day, my eyes brim when I taste them.

45 COOKIES

9 oz (250g) butter or margarine, softened

¾ cup (100g) powdered sugar, plus more for dusting

1 tsp vanilla extract

1 cup (100g) ground almonds (see "Grandma Knows Best")

2 cups (280g) all-purpose flour

Preheat the oven to 325°F (160°C). Line a few baking sheets with parchment paper.

In a mixer fitted with the flat attachment, mix the butter, powdered sugar, vanilla and almonds at medium speed for 2 minutes, until the batter is creamy. Add the flour and mix at low speed just until the dough is homogenous and soft. If the dough is too dry, add 1 tablespoon (15ml) cold water. If it is too sticky, add 1 tablespoon (8g) flour.

Roll the dough into balls, about the size of a cherry tomato. With your finger, make a little indent in the center of each ball, and press a fork around its edges.

Bake for 15–20 minutes, until light golden (the cookies must be light in color). Let cool for a few minutes, and generously dust the still warm cookies with powdered sugar. Cool further before serving. Keep in a closed container at room temperature.

GRANDMA KNOWS BEST

In the old days, you couldn't buy ground almonds (what pastry chefs refer to as "almond flour") in supermarkets; you made them yourself. To do so, blanch almonds in boiling water, until the skins loosen up, and peel them. Dry a little in the oven, until they are golden (mom used to do it in a toaster oven). Cool completely. (That's important! Otherwise, they will turn into marzipan when ground). Grind in a food processor (or the strangely named contraption we had at home—1-2-3). Nowadays, I just buy ready-made almond flour.

Turkish Delight Crescents

These dearly loved and highly nostalgic cookies were originally made with S.F.M. dough (sour cream-flour-margarine). I have since upgraded the recipe, using butter and whipping cream instead of the margarine and sour cream. The cookies are crunchy and have a sweet surprise of Turkish delight in them.

48 COOKIES

2½ cups (350g) self-rising flour

5½ oz (150g) cold butter, diced

1 cup (450ml) whipping cream

About 7 oz (200g) Turkish delight, cut into cubes (see page 209)

Powdered sugar

Preheat the oven to 350°F (180°C). Line a few baking sheets with parchment paper.

In a food processor, process the self-rising flour and butter cubes to a crumbly consistency. Add the whipping cream and mix in short pulses, just until the dough is soft and homogenous.

Divide the dough into 3 equal parts. Roll each part out into a thin (a little less than ¼ inch [6mm]) circle. With a pizza slicer, cut into 16 narrow triangles.

Place a cube of Turkish delight close to the base of each triangle, and roll up like a croissant. Spaciously place the crescents on the prepared baking sheets.

Bake for 15–20 minutes, until light golden. Let cool, dust with powdered sugar and serve.

GRANDMA KNOWS BEST

Turkish delight can be bought or homemade (see page 209).

Roll dough into a thin circle and cut into 16 triangles.

Place a cube of Turkish delight close to the base of each triangle.

Roll up each triangle like a croissant.

WHERE ARE YOU AT THE HOLIDAYS?

So what if they show up only once a year? Here are some sweet delights that are definitely worth the 11+ months' wait.

Where are you on Rosh Hashanah?

Honey Cake

Delicate, moist, soft, fragrant, never-failing . . . I can go on and on with the superlatives. This super-fast honey cake is prepared in a food processor, and the glorious result is always inversely proportional to the amount of work put into it. Another secret is its simple yet magical delicate seasoning. This Rosh Hashanah (New Year) cake is so good, you will find yourself making it all year-round.

2 LOAF CAKES

1 cup (200g) sugar
1¼ cups (300ml) honey, divided
3 eggs
¾ cup (180ml) vegetable oil
1 tsp ground cinnamon
2½ cups (350g) all-purpose flour
1 tbsp (10g) baking powder
1 cup (240ml) very hot dark tea
(brewed with 2 teabags)

Preheat the oven to 325°F (160°C). Grease 2 loaf pans.

In a food processor, process the sugar, 1 cup (240ml) of the honey, eggs, oil and cinnamon for 1 minute, until the batter is airy. Add the flour and baking powder, and mix for another 5 seconds to combine. While mixing, carefully pour in (through the feed tube in the food processor's cover) the hot tea, and mix for another 5 seconds to combine.

Pour the batter into the greased pans, and bake for 40–45 minutes, until the cakes are puffed up, brown and springy to the touch.

Take out of the oven, and drizzle 2 tablespoons (30ml) of the remaining honey on each cake. Wait 1 minute, until the honey heats up and becomes liquid, and spread it with the back of a spoon over the whole cake. Let cool a little before serving. Keep covered at room temperature.

GRANDMA KNOWS BEST

This honey cake is baked at a relatively low temperature to make sure it doesn't rise too much and spill over. A higher temperature might also cause the honey and the sugar in the cake to caramelize and burn.

Where are you breaking the fast?

Rosetta—Refreshing Almond Drink

At the end of the Yom Kippur fast, it is important—and highly recommended—to have a sweet and refreshing drink, even before the traditional tea and cake. This is a mind-and-body rejuvenating beverage: the Tunisian Rosetta, an almond concentrate, is mixed with water and ice before serving. It takes some work, but yields a large amount. You can even prepare it on Rosh Hashanah and keep it in the refrigerator until Yom Kippur. The Rosetta's special flavor comes from a specific, bitter kind of almond (you can get it in specialty markets). If you use regular almonds, add a few drops of almond extract (which can be found in spice shops or specialty stores). To extract the almond concentrate, squeeze the almond pulp through gauze fabric (or a new cloth diaper or a clean cotton shirt you won't need), and "May you all be sealed in the book of life for a good year!"

1 QUART (1L) ALMOND CONCENTRATE

FOR THE ALMOND MIXTURE
3 cups (300g) peeled almonds
½ cup (50g) peeled bitter almonds
3 cups (720ml) water, divided

FOR THE SYRUP
5 cups (1 kg) sugar
2 cups (480ml) water
2 tbsp (30ml) rose water (not extract)

To make the almond mixture, in a food processor, combine all the regular and bitter almonds (see the "Grandma Knows Best" section below) with 1 cup (240ml) of the water. Grind together for 2 minutes. Transfer the mixture to a gauze fabric, and squeeze the liquid into a large pot.

Return what is left in the fabric to the food processor, and add another 1 cup (240ml) of water. Repeat the grinding and squeezing. Repeat the entire process one more time with the remaining 1 cup (240ml) of water. Any remaining ground almonds can be saved for another purpose (they are not needed here, but can be used in other recipes, like the Jam and Crumb Squares on page 141).

To make the syrup, add the sugar and water to the pot with the almond liquid. Heat over medium heat, stirring, until all the sugar has dissolved. Turn the heat up, and bring to a boil. Lower the heat and let simmer for 10 minutes. Remove from the stove, mix in the rose water, let cool and bottle. Keep in the refrigerator.

To serve the drink, mix in a pitcher 1 cup (240ml) of Rosetta with 4 cups (1L) of water, and add ice cubes. Serve immediately.

GRANDMA KNOWS BEST
If you bought almonds in their skin, put them in a bowl, and cover with boiling water. Let sit for a few minutes, until the skins loosen up, and press to peel.

"BREAK" THE FAST
CAKES AND COOKIES FOR A "GOOD SEAL" OF THE DAY

My Mother's Apricot Bow Ties

Every year, my mom whips these babies up as refreshment for the "Ushpizin" (the special Feast of Tabernacles guests). Puff pastry, apricot jam and a little sugar, and you got yourself some caramelized and crispy cookies to snack on. It is uncanny that these three simple ingredients produce such a great delight (I have tried it with other jams, but apricot is the best).

30 COOKIES

30 squares of puff pastry, defrosted (you can use a pre-rolled pastry, and cut it into 30 squares)
1 cup (240g) apricot jam
½ cup (100g) sugar

Preheat the oven to 375°F (190°C). Line a few baking sheets with parchment paper.

Working with each pastry square individually, spread a teaspoon of jam on half of the square. Fold the other half over—you get a jam-filled rectangle. Cut a lengthwise line down the middle of the rectangle, leaving about 1 inch (2.5cm) on either end. Fold the upper half of the rectangle over and pull through the slit, to create the twisted shape. Place on the prepared baking sheet, and generously sprinkle with sugar.

Bake for about 25 minutes, until golden. Let cool a little before serving (careful, the jam is boiling!). Eat on the day of baking.

Spread jam on half of the square and fold the other half over.

Cut a lengthwise line down the middle of the rectangle.

Pull the slit apart a little.

Fold the upper half of the rectangle over and pull through the slit.

Stretch to create the twisted shape.

Sprinkle with sugar and until golden.

Hanukkah Doughnuts (Sufganiyot)

This is a secret recipe in many pastry shops I know. Apparently, it is based on some grandmother's recipe that goes way back, so far back, in fact, that I couldn't find an actual name to go with it (or to give the well-deserved credit to). As per tradition, it is also very delicious and happily inexpensive (which would explain why the pastry shops are so willing to sell it). Even homemade, these doughnuts are like perfectly round, soft and fluffy pillows. Don't be offended if your family and guests don't believe they are not store-bought.

30 DOUGHNUTS

FOR THE DOUGHNUTS

7 cups (1kg) all-purpose flour, divided, plus more for dusting

2 tbsp (17g) active dry yeast

1¼ cups (300ml) lukewarm milk

½ cup (100g) granulated sugar

3 eggs

3½ oz (100g) butter, softened

2 tbsp (30ml) brandy

Zest of ½ lemon

1½ qt (1.5L) vegetable oil, for deep-frying

Strawberry jam, for filling

Powdered sugar, for dusting

To make the doughnuts, in a mixer fitted with the kneading attachment, add about half of the flour, and mix in the yeast. Add the milk, granulated sugar, eggs, butter, brandy and lemon zest, and mix for 1 minute, until the batter is homogenous and loose.

Gradually add the remaining half of the flour, mixing at low speed. Turn the speed up to medium, and knead for another 5 minutes, until the dough is smooth and shiny. Cover the bowl with plastic wrap, and set aside to rise until the dough doubles in bulk, 1–2 hours.

Transfer the dough to a very lightly floured work surface, and make 30 egg-size balls. (How to divide by 30? Simple. First, divide the dough into 3 equal parts. Now roll each part into a long "sausage." Cut the sausage in half, and divide each half into 5 parts.) Put the balls on a greased sheet of parchment paper, or on individual parchment paper squares (see the "Grandma Knows Best" section below). Cover with greased plastic wrap, greased side down, to prevent drying.

Set aside to rise until doubled in bulk, 1–2 hours.

In a wide pot, heat the oil to 325°F (160°C) on a deep-frying thermometer. Deep-fry the doughnuts, 4 or 5 at a time, for about 2 minutes on each side, until brown. If you use the paper squares method, you can put the doughnuts in the oil with them. Remove the cooked doughnuts with a spider or tongs, and put them on a paper towel to soak up the oil. Place the jam in a pastry bag fitted with a long, narrow tip. Inject the doughnuts with jam, generously dust with powdered sugar and serve.

GRANDMA KNOWS BEST

Here is a sweet secret I learned from Chef Oren Giron to ensure that the dough balls do not lose their shape when transferred to the pot: Put the dough balls on precut, individual parchment paper squares and let them rise. When they are ready to be fried, simply pick them up with the paper and put them in the oil (with the paper). No need to fuss with the paper; it will separate from the dough on its own after a few seconds of frying. Use tongs—and extreme caution—to take them out.

Sfenj

I was never able to pronounce the name of this pastry correctly. *Sfenj* actually means "sponge," and these are indeed spongy, springy and full of air bubbles. I learned this recipe from my friend and pastry chef Ruta, and here it is, with a few minor adjustments. In my family, sfenj are consumed in three different ways: mom likes them plain; most of the family (including yours truly) prefer them sugar-coated; and my own private chef heats up some honey in the microwave oven and dips them between bites. Allow for at least two sfenj per person; I am yet to meet anybody who can stop at one.

25 LARGE SFENJ

7 cups (1kg) all-purpose flour

2 tbsp (17g) active dry yeast

½ cup (100g) sugar, plus more for rolling

½ tsp salt

3⅓ cups (800ml) lukewarm water, divided

1½ qt (1.5L) vegetable oil, for deep-frying

GRANDMA KNOWS BEST

Sfenj must be prepared and fried when they are meant to be served. Don't prepare this dough ahead of time, and don't put it in the refrigerator. When cold, it is hard to work with, and it goes sour very quickly (within 4 hours).

In the largest bowl you have, mix the flour and yeast. Add the sugar and salt, and mix with the flour. Pour in about half the water, and begin kneading with your hands—fingers spread open, using lifting motions from the bottom of the bowl to the surface of the dough. Gradually add (all!) the remaining water, and knead for another minute, and no more! This dough must not be over-kneaded. It is very loose, and that's okay.

Cover in plastic wrap and set aside to rise, until doubled in bulk. With very wet (dripping with water) hands, work the dough to let out the air (it will return to its original volume). Cover, and let rise again until doubled in bulk. This second rising will be a lot shorter, so you may begin heating up your oil. In a wide pot, heat the oil to 325°F (160°C) on a deep-frying thermometer.

Dip your hands in a bowl of cold oil or water. Pinch a ball of dough (tangerine size) and pull it up. With your other hand, pinch under it to cut it off the rest of the dough. Holding the ball of dough with both hands, insert your finger in its center to create a hole, and stretch until the hole is about 1½ inches (3.8cm) in diameter. Carefully place the bagel shape into the hot oil. Repeat with the rest of the dough (not forgetting to dip your hands in cold oil or water occasionally).

Deep-fry until sfenj are golden, 2–3 minutes on each side. Put the fried sfenj on a paper towel to soak up the excess oil. Dip each sfenj in a bowl of sugar to coat, and serve immediately.

Pinch a ball of dough.

Create a hole in the middle.

Carefully place into the hot oil.

Matzah and Chocolate Layer Cake

Admittedly, matzah shmeared with a thick layer of chocolate spread is hands-down the best Pesach (Passover) food. Using the same indulgent concept, this chocolaty construction of alternate layers of matzah dipped in coffee and a yummy chocolate mousse is a very close second (with matzah brei coming in at third place, if you must know).

25 BITE-SIZE TREATS

11 oz (300g) dark chocolate, chopped

2 cups (480ml) whipping cream, divided

1 cup (240ml) lukewarm coffee (without milk or sugar)

5 matzahs

In a microwave-safe bowl, combine the chunks of dark chocolate and 1¼ cups (300ml) of the whipping cream. Heat in a microwave oven until melted, and whisk to a homogenous cream. Cool to room temperature. Set aside half of the mixture (about 1 cup [240ml]) for the frosting.

In a mixer, beat the remaining ¾ cup (180ml) whipping cream to soft peaks. Add to the remaining chocolate mixture in the bowl, and fold to a homogenous mousse.

Pour the coffee into a wide and flat tray. Dip the two sides of each matzah in the coffee for 30 seconds.

Put a coffee-soaked matzah on the bottom of a serving tray, and spread with one-forth of the chocolate mousse. Lay the second matzah and spread another one-fourth of the mousse. Repeat until you have assembled a "tower" of 5 matzahs and chocolate mousse (the top layer will be matzah). Spread the top matzah with the reserved chocolate frosting (if it is too hard, heat a little in a microwave oven).

Cover and transfer to the refrigerator for 4 hours, for the chocolate to set and the matzahs to soften. Cut into squares and serve cold.

AND ANOTHER THING

Want more ideas for Passover? Flip ahead to the Passover Festive Chocolate-Coconut Cake (page 183) and Abambar cookies (page 184).

GRANDMA KNOWS BEST

For a pareve (dairy-free) version, use nondairy whipping cream and nondairy dark chocolate.

If you insist on the authentic olden-day taste, dip the matzahs in sweet red wine instead of coffee.

The best serving tray for this cake is the matzah dish. If you don't have one, any box/pan of the right size will do, and if you don't have that, assemble the cake on a double sheet of aluminum foil.

Passover Festive Chocolate-Coconut Cake

Forget the dry and dense Pesach cakes! With a baked (and moist!) coconut base, a rich (and fast) chocolate mousse filling and a sweet whipped cream frosting, this cake will really make Pesach a happy holiday. For a pareve version (great as a dessert after the seder), substitute the butter with margarine, the dairy whipping cream with a nondairy one, and make sure the chocolate is nondairy, too.

ONE 9¾-INCH (24-CM) CAKE

FOR THE COCONUT LAYER
6 egg whites, at room temperature (save the yolks for the chocolate layer)
1 cup (200g) sugar
2 cups (200g) desiccated coconut

FOR THE CHOCOLATE LAYER
7 oz (200g) dark chocolate
3½ tbsp (50g) butter
6 egg yolks

FOR THE WHIPPED CREAM
2 cups (480ml) whipping cream
¼ cup (50g) sugar
2 tbsp (20g) vanilla-flavored instant pudding mix

Preheat the oven to 350°F (180°C). Grease a 9½-inch (24-cm) springform pan.

To make the coconut layer, in a mixer, beat the egg whites at medium speed for 1 minute, until they turn to a white soft froth with large bubbles. Gradually add the sugar, and beat until the meringue is firm and shiny. Add the desiccated coconut to the meringue, and fold with a spatula, until incorporated. Spread in the greased pan, and bake for about 30 minutes, until golden. Set aside to cool.

To make the chocolate layer, in a microwave-safe bowl, melt the chocolate and butter in a microwave oven. Mix in the egg yolks and heat for another 10 seconds to get rid of any bacteria in the yolks. Stir until combined, and set aside for 5 minutes to cool.

To make the whipped cream, in a mixer, beat the whipping cream, sugar and pudding mix to soft peaks.

Add half of the whipped cream to the lukewarm chocolate mixture, and fold until the mousse is homogenous. Spread the mousse over the baked coconut base. Gently spread the remaining whipped cream over the chocolate layer.

Put in the refrigerator for 2 hours to set. Slice with a knife dipped in boiling water (dipping and wiping dry between cuts).

GRANDMA KNOWS BEST

The chocolate cream contains uncooked egg yolks, so in order to "kill off" any salmonella, I heat it in the microwave oven. If you prefer your mousse without eggs altogether, refer to the Chocolate Mousse without Eggs recipe on page 43 (saving the yolks for something else).

Abambar—Libyan Almond Cookies

Abambar are Tripolitanian almond cookies I found in the Netanya market, where they are sold year-round but especially for Passover. The abambar resemble macaroons, but are less delicate in look and texture. They are cracked and tanned, taste like marzipan and have the unique aroma of bitter almonds. After much trial and error, I came to the conclusion that simple is best: store-bought ground almonds, regular meringue and a little cornstarch. So (drum roll, please . . .) here are my homemade abambar!

40 LARGE COOKIES

18 oz (500g) peeled ground almonds

3⅓ cups (400g) powdered sugar

3 egg whites

1 tsp cornstarch

1 tsp almond essence (or 10 bitter almonds, finely ground)

40 peeled almonds

Preheat the oven to 350°F (180°C). Line a few baking sheets with parchment paper.

In a bowl, mix together the ground almonds and powdered sugar.

In a mixer, beat the egg whites at medium speed to get a firm meringue.

Replace the beating attachment with a flat one. Add the almond mixture, cornstarch and almond essence to the meringue. Beat at medium speed for 1 minute, to get a soft, marzipan-like dough (it can keep in the refrigerator overnight before shaping and baking).

With wet hands, shape into balls (ping-pong ball size), and spaciously lay on the prepared baking sheets. Gently press an almond into the center of each ball for garnish.

Bake for 15 minutes, until the balls flatten down, crack a bit and turn gold (don't overbake!). The cookies should still be soft when taken out of the oven; they set when cooled.

Cool completely before attempting to lift the cookies off the paper, which should be peeled off ever so gently, because the cookies tend to stick to it. Keep in a closed container at room temperature.

GRANDMA KNOWS BEST

The almond essence is what gives these cookies their signature fragrance—it is made with a specific kind of small, shriveled and extremely bitter almond. If you want, you may substitute the almond essence with 10 bitter almonds, very (very) finely grounded (bitter almonds can be found in spice shops).

Mufleta

No Mimouna, the North African post-Passover celebration, is worthy of its name if you don't serve mufleta, a Moroccan flat pastry. The Moroccan Mimouna is traditionally celebrated on the night and day after Passover, but you don't have to come from Moroccan ancestry to enjoy it or even to produce perfect mufleta (although in my case it definitely helped). Strictly follow the instructions, and yours will be perfect, too. Put some Moroccan music on full blast, open your front door to let passersby in and don't forget to bless them with the traditional *Tarbakhu utsa'adu* ("May you enjoy prosperity and good fortune").

40 MUFLETA

7 cups (1kg) all-purpose flour

1 tsp salt

2½ cups (600ml) water, plus more as needed

2 cups (480ml) vegetable oil

Butter and honey, for serving

Chocolate spread, for serving

In a mixer fitted with the kneading attachment, combine the flour and salt. Add the water, and mix at medium speed for 10 minutes, until the dough is smooth, shiny, elastic, and sticky. If it is little hard, gradually add ¼ cup (60ml) more water.

Divide the dough into 40 equal parts (see the "Grandma Knows Best" section below), and shape them into ping-pong size balls.

Pour the oil into a bowl and roll each ball in the oil, until coated on all sides. Spaciously place the oiled balls on a tray. Pour the remaining oil over them (to prevent drying). Set aside for 1 hour at room temperature.

Preheat a large frying pan over medium heat.

Spread some of the oil on the work surface, and put a dough ball on it. With the palms of your hands, in spreading motions, "open" the ball (you should "caress" the dough in all directions to stretch it), until it is a flat, even circle (if it tears a little, no big deal!).

Place the stretched-out dough in the hot frying pan (no need to grease the pan—there's plenty of oil in the mufleta). Peek under to see if it is golden, and turn.

Meanwhile, prepare the next one, and place over the one already in the pan. Fry like this for half a minute, until golden, and turn the two together. Now the second mufleta is face down in the pan.

Place a new one on the two, wait half a minute until golden, turn the whole stack over and place a new one on top. Repeat until the stack of mufleta is 10–12 high. With the exception of the first mufleta, they are all fried on one side only, but the heat inside the stack cooks them all through. Put the stack of mufleta on a plate and cover with a towel to keep warm. Start a new stack.

Serve with butter and honey (for children of all ages, serve chocolate spread too).

GRANDMA KNOWS BEST

This recipe makes 40 beautiful mufleta. To divide it into 40 equal parts, roll the dough into a ball, and cut it into 4 equal parts. Roll each quarter into a "sausage," cut each sausage in half, and cut each half into 5 parts.

MORE IDEAS FOR THE MIMOUNA TABLE

Here are some other sweet treats to grace your Mimouna table:

Cheese and Raisins Blintzes

On Shavuot of last year, all records were broken! I had brought all the desserts to the table and went to the kitchen to get a knife for the cake. When I returned to the dining table five seconds later, all the blintzes were G-O-N-E! So, knowing full well that I don't stand a chance to eat one at the table, I pull an all-you-can-eat buffet when I make them. The crepes are suitable for both sweet and savory fillings, but nothing beats the simplest, nostalgic sweet cheese, lemon zest and raisins version (with a little pudding mix to firm it up). The batter makes thirteen crepes, but as you know, the first one almost always "fails," so you will have what is known as "the baker's dozen."

12 PLUMP BLINTZES

FOR THE BLINTZES (CREPES)

3 eggs

½ tsp salt

1 cup (240ml) water

1 cup (240ml) milk

3 tbsp (45ml) vegetable oil

1½ cups (210g) all-purpose flour

Butter for frying

FOR THE CHEESE AND RAISIN FILLING

1 cup (250g) cream cheese

1 cup (250g) ricotta cheese

¼ cup (50g) sugar

¼ cup (40g) vanilla-flavored instant pudding mix

Zest of ½ lemon

¾ cup (100g) raisins

Honey, for drizzling

To make the blintzes, in a blender or a food processor, combine the eggs, salt, water, milk, oil and flour, and mix for 1 minute, until the batter is smooth and lump-free. If you do this part manually, put the flour, water and milk in a bowl, and whisk for 2 minutes. Add the eggs, oil and salt, and whisk for another 1 minute to combine.

Sift the batter. This is very important; there are always tiny lumps of flour.

Grease a large nonstick frying pan (10–11 inches [25–28cm] in diameter) with oil spray or a little butter (you can use an electric fryer).

Pour half a ladle of batter into the pan, and immediately tilt it in a circular motion to evenly distribute the batter. Cook only until the face of the crepe looks dry, the edges lift a little and the bottom begins to turn gold. Don't turn over! Blintzes are fried on one side only. Repeat with the remaining batter, occasionally greasing the pan. Stack the blintzes on a plate, and set aside to cool.

To make the filling, in a bowl, whisk together the cream cheese, ricotta cheese, sugar, pudding mix and lemon zest, until the mixture is homogenous and lump-free. Fold in the raisins.

Place each blintz on the work surface, un-fried side up. Place a heaping tablespoon (15g) of filling in a strip across its center. Fold the sides over the strip of filling (to "lock" it in), and roll into a roulade.

Keep in the refrigerator for up to 2–3 days. They are already great, but they will be even better if you fry them in butter on both sides, until golden, and serve them hot, with a drizzle of honey.

GRANDMA KNOWS BEST

If you made a double amount and don't want to fry all of the already rolled-up blintzes, you can arrange them tightly in a paper-lined baking tray, brush with melted butter and bake at 400°F (200°C) for 10 minutes, until they are hot and have gotten a little crispy.

Ricotta and Chocolate Puff Pastry "Pages"

Looks complicated? At first, I couldn't figure out how to make this gorgeous Italian pastry, traditionally called sfogliatella (pronounced sfo-lia-tella). However, once you get the idea, it is really easy. Southern Italian grandmothers make it with strips of dough rolled out in a pasta machine until translucent. I cheat. I make it with phyllo pastry. You brush the pastry with melted butter and make a roulade, adding phyllo sheets as you go, until the roulade is plump and chubby. The roulade is sliced, and each slice is folded into a pouch and filled with ricotta cheese (in honor of Shavuot's traditional dairy menu) and chocolate. In the oven, the "pages" separate and the magic happens. No way can I wait for these delicacies to cool—I devour them straight out of the oven with loud crunchy bites.

20 PASTRIES

18 oz (500g) phyllo pastry, defrosted

5½ oz (150g) melted butter, at room temperature

1 cup (250g) ricotta cheese

3½ oz (100g) dark chocolate, coarsely chopped

Powdered sugar, for dusting

GRANDMA KNOWS BEST

These pastries can be filled with quality cheese fillings or you can bake them without any filling at all (in which case, put a ball of aluminum foil in the pouch to keep them open). After baking, cool, take the aluminum foil ball out and pipe a little whipped cream in.

Line your work surface with a sheet of parchment paper, and put a phyllo pastry sheet on it. Thoroughly brush the pastry with melted butter, and roll into a tight roulade. Use the paper to start rolling (the first is the most delicate and difficult; it gets easier down the road).

Set the roulade aside, and thoroughly brush another sheet of phyllo pastry with melted butter. Place the first roulade along the edge of the second sheet, and roll them together tightly into a now thicker roulade. Repeat with all the phyllo sheets, making sure you roll in the same direction every time. See the photos below.

Preheat the oven to 400°F (200°C). Line a baking sheet with parchment paper.

Slice the phyllo roulade into ⅔-inch (1.5-cm) thick slices. Lay each slice on the work surface, and flatten gently with your hand. Hold the flattened slice between your thumb and forefinger, and begin pushing the center out, to form a pouch (like kibbeh). You will get a cone-shaped "hat."

In a bowl, combine the ricotta cheese and chopped chocolate. Put a teaspoon of the filling in the pouch, and pinch the edges to close (it will open slightly during baking, and that's okay). Repeat with all the pastry cones, and lay on the prepared baking sheet.

Bake for 10 minutes, until browned. Let cool a little, dust with powdered sugar and serve. The pastry maintains its freshness only on the day it is made. You can do all the prebaking stages and freeze. When you are ready to bake them, they go straight from the freezer to the oven—no need to defrost.

Slice the phyllo roulade into thick slices.

Gently flatten then push the center out to form a pouch.

Fill and pinch the edges to close.

I WANT CANDY

You wouldn't believe the classic and nostalgic flavors I have re-created at home!

Candied Apple on a Stick

It took many trials (and errors) to get this beloved treat right. I learned some valuable lessons along that bumpy road, the most important being:

- Really and thoroughly scrub and dry every apple. Apparently, there is a coating of wax on them, and you must get rid of all of it if you want the caramel to stick.
- Cook your syrup to a near-caramel, but don't let it turn gold. The coating must remain clear.
- You need the corn syrup; it gives the candied apples a longer "shelf life" (before they melt, which is the end of every candied apple).
- One last—and important—sweet secret: Do not make candied apples on a damp day (unless you plan to eat them immediately); they will melt and become too sticky. If you make them in better, more temperate weather (not too damp and not too hot), wrapped in cellophane, they keep nicely for about 3 days.

6 CANDIED APPLES

6 Granny Smith apples

6 short, thick skewers, to stick in the apples

4 cups (800g) sugar

1½ cups (360ml) water

1 cup (320g) corn syrup

A few drops of red food coloring (optional)

First and foremost, thoroughly scrub the apples with a scrubber sponge, warm water and soap. Rinse and dry (again—thoroughly). Insert a thick skewer into the center of each apple, at least 1¼ inches (3cm) deep.

Line a baking pan with a sheet of parchment paper and grease the paper; this is where you will put the apples after coating. Prepare a large pot, pan or deep tray to hold about 1 inch (2.5cm) of ice water to cool the pot in after cooking.

In a large pot, bring the sugar, water and corn syrup to a boil. Cook over medium heat for about 10 minutes, until the bubbles begin to disappear, the syrup is sticky but still clear and it is just beginning to change color to gold. At this point, almost all the water has evaporated, and caramel is about to form. This is 300°F (150°C) on a candy thermometer. If you don't have one, drip a few drops of the syrup into a cup with cold water—it is ready when the syrup drops turn to little "glass" balls.

Remove from the stove, and put the cooking pot in the container with ice water for a few seconds to stop the cooking process. Add the food coloring, if desired.

Holding the skewer, dip each apple into the syrup (careful, it's hot!) to coat it all. Dip only once. Toward the end, when the level of syrup in the pot is lower, you may need to tilt the pot to coat the whole apple in one go. Let any excess syrup drip back into the pot, and place the coated apple "on its head," skewer sticking up, on the greased paper.

Repeat with all the apples. If the caramel cools and hardens a little, reheat it over low heat, until it is hot and liquid again.

Let the candied apples cool at room temperature. Serve immediately, or wrap each apple in cellophane (not just for looks—it protects the coating from moisture) and keep at room temperature.

GRANDMA KNOWS BEST

Got something against food coloring? Here is a great tip for you (from this book's awesome editor, Ms. Moran Amrami Rozenboim): Prepare the apples without the food coloring, and instead of wrapping them in the usual clear cellophane, wrap them in red cellophane.

AND GRANDMA WOULD SAY

It is important to dip the apple only one time. Dipped twice or more, the caramel layer will be too thick and tooth breaking.

Sweet Popcorn

As a child, I bought a bag of sweet popcorn that must have been on the shelf of Hananya's grocery store for many months. One fistful was enough to turn me off it for a long, long time. Many years later, however, returning from a trip to America, my parents brought back many different snacks, among which was a box of sweet popcorn I just couldn't stop munching on. Well, you know me—I decided to try to make it at home. A perfect result the first time! I have since been making it a lot. (Wholesale proportions! It keeps for a long time in a closed container.)

A LITTLE OVER 2 POUNDS (1KG) COATED POPCORN

FOR THE POPCORN
¼ cup (60ml) vegetable oil
1 cup (200g) popcorn kernels

FOR THE SWEET CARAMEL COATING
7 oz (200g) butter
1 cup (200g) granulated sugar
1 cup (240g) firmly packed dark brown sugar
½ cup (120ml) honey
1 tsp lemon juice
1 tsp salt
1 tsp vanilla extract
½ tsp baking soda

To make the popcorn, pour the oil into a large pot and add 3 or 4 popcorn kernels. Heat the oil over high heat. After about 2 minutes, the kernels will pop—that's the time to add the rest of the popcorn kernels (in a single layer—if necessary, do this in batches), and immediately cover the pot.

Keep cooking until the frequency of popping sounds drops and you can count to 3 between pops. Remove from the heat, and transfer the popcorn to the largest bowl you have (getting rid of any unpopped kernels).

To make the sweet caramel coating, in a large pot (this is important, because toward the end of the cooking process, the mixture rises), combine the butter, granulated sugar, brown sugar, honey, lemon juice, salt and vanilla, and heat over medium heat, stirring, until the mixture is perfectly smooth and all the sugar granules have dissolved. Turn up the heat to medium-high, and boil without stirring, until the mixture thickens a little. If you have a candy thermometer, it should reach just under 300°F (150°C). If you don't have one, this takes 3 minutes on high heat or 8 minutes on low heat. Whatever you do, keep a close eye on your pot, because the mixture burns easily.

Remove from the stove, and carefully (!) mix in the baking soda. The mixture will bubble and rise like crazy. Immediately, pour the boiling caramel over the popcorn, and mix with two large spoons, until all the popcorn is coated.

Next, you'll dry the coated popcorn in the oven. Preheat the oven to 250°F (120°C). Line 2 baking sheets with parchment paper.

Spread the popcorn mixture in the pans, and dry in the oven for about 1 hour. Let cool, gently separate the popcorn with your hands and serve. Keep in a closed container at room temperature.

GRANDMA KNOWS BEST

When you buy the popcorn kernels, make sure they are plump and shiny for a perfect popping percentage—the small, shriveled ones don't pop.

AND GRANDMA WOULD SAY

To clean the pot after making the caramel, fill it with water (add the mixing spoons while you are at it), cover and boil for 5 minutes, and—voilà—any residual caramel in the pot has magically melted and vanished.

Pink Coconut Bar

If you ask people in Israel what is the most nostalgic candy bar of their childhood, most will answer without hesitation: "pink coconut!" I am so happy I was successful in re-creating its sweetness and moistness in a homemade version. The signature pink color comes from raspberry concentrate (which in and of itself is a childhood flavor). This coconut bar can be eaten on the day of preparation, but its texture and taste improve after a night in the refrigerator, during which the coconut flakes absorb the condensed milk, the bars set and it all becomes even moister.

ABOUT 20 BARS

FOR THE WHITE COCONUT MIXTURE
½ cup (120ml) water

3½ tbsp (50g) butter

1 (14 oz [400g]) can condensed milk

3 cups (300g) desiccated coconut

FOR THE PINK COCONUT COATING
1½ cups (150g) desiccated coconut

¼ cup (60ml) red raspberry concentrate or malabi syrup

To make the coconut mixture, in a large pot over medium heat, combine the water, butter and condensed milk and bring to a boil. Cook for another 2 minutes. The mixture will bubble and seem like it is going to overflow. As long as your pot is large enough, this should be okay. Remove from the stove, add the desiccated coconut, and stir until the mixture is doughy, soft and moist. Let cool to room temperature.

Spread a "line" of a one-fourth of the mixture across a sheet of parchment paper, and create a 1¼-inch (3-cm) thick cylinder. This mixture doesn't lend itself to rolling. In order to shape it, press with your hands, like a snake, or use the "ruler technique" in the "Grandma Knows Best" section below. Repeat with the remaining mixture to create a total of 4 cylinders. Put in the refrigerator for 2 hours, or in the freezer for 30 minutes, to set.

To make the pink coconut coating, rub the desiccated coconut with the raspberry concentrate with your fingers, until all the coconut is "dyed" pink. Spread the pink coconut on a baking sheet.

Peel the parchment paper off the coconut cylinders and roll them (apply a little pressure) in the pink desiccated coconut—the moist coating will adhere to the coconut cylinders.

Cut the cylinders into units (bite-size "coins" or 2½-inch [6.5cm] bars, like the store-bought variety). Keep covered in the refrigerator. Serve cold or at room temperature.

GRANDMA KNOWS BEST
Rather than rolling this uncooperative mixture by hand, which entails cooling and hardening it in the refrigerator, use a ruler to shape it while it is still malleable: Form a long "snake" of the mixture across the center of a sheet of parchment paper. Fold the paper in half over the mixture. Place a ruler over the paper, against the snake. Pull the bottom half of the paper toward you, while pressing the ruler down toward the work surface. The mixture will be packed between the paper and the ruler into a perfect cylinder. This technique is suitable for other mixtures, including cookie doughs.

Homemade Marshmallow

Grandmothers always say, "No need to go out and buy, I'll make it at home, and it will be even better," and they happen to be right: Homemade marshmallows are soft as a cloud and melt in your mouth. They are not too sweet, and I only make white ones—no food coloring. Marshmallows are made with whipped egg whites, boiling syrup and gelatin, and if you follow the instructions to the letter, it is no trouble at all. A candy thermometer is useful here, but you can manage without it.

FIFTY 2-INCH (5-CM) MARSHMALLOWS

FOR THE COATING
1 cup (120g) powdered sugar
1 cup (140g) cornstarch

FOR THE GELATIN
1 oz (28g) gelatin powder
1 tbsp (12g) granulated sugar
1 tsp vanilla extract
½ cup (120ml) water

FOR THE SYRUP
2 cups (400g) granulated sugar
¾ cup (180ml) water

FOR THE MERINGUE
2 egg whites

To make the coating, mix together the powdered sugar and cornstarch. Line a large oven tray with a sheet of parchment paper. Sift 3-4 tablespoons (24-32g) of the powdered sugar and cornstarch mixture over the paper. Save the rest to coat the cooked marshmallow later.

To make the gelatin, combine the gelatin powder, granulated sugar and vanilla in a bowl. Pour the water into a separate, microwave-safe bowl, and then sprinkle the gelatin mixture on top. Set aside to dissolve.

To make the syrup, in a large pot over medium heat, heat the granulated sugar and water, stirring, until the sugar is dissolved. Bring to a boil, and cook for about 7 minutes, without stirring, until the bubbles are smaller and the syrup is rubbery—250°F (120°C) on a candy thermometer. Another way to test the syrup is to drip ½ teaspoon of syrup into a cup of cold water. If it turns into a clear and elastic ball between your fingers, it is ready.

When the syrup is almost cooked, make the meringue. Beat the egg whites in a mixer, at high speed, to get a soft white froth.

Heat the gelatin mixture in the microwave oven for 15-20 seconds, until melted. Place next to the mixer.

When the syrup reaches 250°F (120°C), remove from the stove. Drizzle the syrup into the mixer, while beating at high speed (careful—it is HOT!). Add the melted gelatin immediately to the mixer. Keep beating for another 10-15 minutes, until the meringue is fluffy, elastic and shining white, and the bowl is no longer hot to the touch (if—and only if—you do want to add food coloring, now is the time).

Spread a 1¼-inch (3-cm) thick layer of the meringue in the prepared pan. Work quickly; it hardens in seconds. Set aside to set at room temperature, uncovered, overnight.

The next day, sprinkle some of the powdered sugar mixture on a work surface. With a knife, release the edges of the marshmallow from the pan, turn over onto the work surface and peel off the parchment paper. Sprinkle more powdered sugar mixture over the marshmallow, until completely covered.

Cut into squares or with a cookie cutter (dipped first in the powdered sugar mixture to prevent sticking). Serve immediately, or keep in a closed container at room temperature (in the summer, keep in the refrigerator).

GRANDMA KNOWS BEST

The marshmallow meringue requires precision and speed, and the mixture is very hot, so this is no job for children. However, after it has cooled and is ready to be cut, the whole family can join (especially since the little ones are allowed to sample the dough in this case).

See Shira and Ariel cutting and eating marshmallows, and messing up the kitchen and me—what fun! Shira is my niece (Ronen's sister's daughter), and Ariel is Moran and Daniel Lailah's son (Moran is my pastry chef friend, and Daniel did the photography for this book).

Soft Caramel Toffee

Who said you can't make caramel toffees without caramel? A little Israeli chutzpah and a lot of experimentation helped me find a winning "non-caramel" caramel toffee, made with sweetened condensed milk and corn syrup. They taste exactly like "Werther's Original," but have a softer, more toffee-like texture. You can snack on them as they are, or turn them into a fancy and elegant sweet, with a coating of chocolate and chopped nuts (to which you can add some coarse salt if you are a salty-and-sweet person). If you prefer hard candy—no problem! Take a peek at the "Grandma Knows Best" section below, and learn how to make them from the same ingredients, but slightly different.

NINETY 1½-INCH (3.8-CM) CARAMELS

7 oz (200g) butter, diced

1 cup (200g) granulated sugar

1 cup (240g) packed brown sugar

1 tbsp (15ml) vanilla extract

1 (14 oz [400g]) can sweetened condensed milk

1 cup (320g) corn syrup

Line 3 loaf pans with parchment paper, and grease the paper.

In a large pot (this is crucial, because the mixture rises when boiling), heat the butter cubes, granulated sugar, brown sugar, vanilla, condensed milk and corn syrup over medium heat, stirring, until the sugars have dissolved completely. Turn up the heat, and bring to a boil. Cook at boiling level, stirring occasionally, for 10–12 minutes, until the mixture thickens and is the color of light dulce de leche (250°F [120°C] on a candy thermometer). Another way to test the syrup is to drip ½ teaspoon of the toffee into a cup of cold water. If it turns into a golden and elastic ball, and feels like modeling clay between your fingers, it is ready.

Remove from the heat, and immediately and carefully (it's HOT!) pour into the prepared pans. Let cool a little, and then put in the refrigerator for 2 hours to further cool and set.

Release from the pans, cut with a sharp knife into little squares, and serve at room temperature. Wrap each candy in parchment paper, and keep at room temperature (in the summer, keep in the refrigerator).

GRANDMA KNOWS BEST

If you undercook (failing to bring the mixture up to 250°F [120°C]), you'll get a delicious runny toffee, which can be used as a sauce. Alternatively, you can return the pot to the stove, and bring the mixture up to a soft toffee consistency (250°F [120°C]). If, however, you have overcooked the mixture (to just under 300°F [150°C]), you'll get some yummy, hard, sucking toffees, from which there is no turning back. So, if you want soft, remember to take the pot off the heat 2–3 minutes earlier, and if your heart is set on hard candy, allow the mixture to reach just under 300°F (150°C), and cut the toffee while it is still hot, before it hardens.

Homemade Marzipan

This is how you make real marzipan without a meat grinder, without double grinding the almonds and sugar and even without blanching, peeling and drying the almonds: you just mix store-bought ground almonds and hot sugar syrup in a blender. The resulting marzipan is very easy to mold and shape, and is good for many things. Me—I like to make bite-size sweets with little patterns imprinted in them (see the photo to the left). Put each sweet in its own paper liner, pack in a box, and give it as a beautiful and tasty homemade gift.

A LITTLE MORE THAN 2 POUNDS (1 KG) MARZIPAN

4 cups (400g) finely ground blanched almonds

1 tsp almond essence (or rose essence or vanilla extract)

1 tsp lemon juice

2¼ cups (450g) granulated sugar

¾ cup (180ml) water

Powdered sugar, to help set the marzipan

In a mixer fitted with the flat attachment, combine the ground almonds, almond essence and lemon juice.

In a large pot over medium heat, heat the granulated sugar and water, stirring, until the sugar is dissolved completely. Bring to a boil, turn the heat to low and cook without stirring for 5 minutes, until the syrup thickens a little. Remove from the stove.

Turn the mixer on low speed, and slowly pour in the hot syrup (careful, it's HOT!). Mix on low speed for another 5 minutes, until the mixture turns to a short-crust pastry-like dough.

Take the dough out of the mixer and work it with your hands to a shiny and elastic marzipan, which is supposed to be a little sticky (it will dry up and crystallize later). If it is too sticky, knead it a little with powdered sugar. If, however, the marzipan is too dry, wet your hands with some water or lemon juice and knead it.

The marzipan is ready! You can keep it in plastic wrap at room temperature to use later, or follow the instructions here, and shape marzipan sweets straight away.

Roll some of the marzipan into small balls (keeping the rest wrapped, because it tends to dry out very quickly—in which case, knead it with wet hands as explained above). You can imprint special patters with store-bought or personalized templates. Roll them in some powdered sugar first to prevent sticking.

Keep the sweets in individual paper liners in a closed container, at room temperature.

GRANDMA KNOWS BEST

This is another way to enjoy marzipan: Roll the marzipan into balls, and dip them in chocolate. Melt 7 ounces (200g) dark chocolate, insert a toothpick in the marzipan ball, pick it up and dip it in the melted chocolate. Place the chocolate-coated marzipan balls on a paper-lined baking sheet, and pull out the toothpick. Freeze for 5 minutes, so the chocolate will set, and transfer to a serving plate.

Homemade Halva

They always stare at me in the supermarket—big halva blocks, coated in chocolate or covered with green pistachios. I decide to buy a large slice with pistachios (for baking, of course), but by the time I get home, only crumbs are left, which I gather in the palm of my hand and inhale. If, like me, you are a halva freak, you must try this recipe, because homemade halva is way better than the store-bought version. It can be made with any type of raw, unseasoned tahini, even the whole-grain sesame tahini. Add anything you like—nuts, roasted almonds, chopped coffee beans, chopped caramelized pecans or chocolate flakes (which will melt a little when the halva is hot). The best way is to prepare a selection of flavors to show off . . . and to sample a little . . . and a little more . . .

1 LOAF PAN

2 cups plus 1 tbsp (500g) raw tahini

2½ cups (500g) sugar

1 cup (240ml) water

1 tbsp (15ml) vanilla extract

1 cup (100g) peeled, roasted and unsalted pistachio nuts

Line a loaf pan with parchment paper, and grease the paper.

Put the raw tahini in a mixer fitted with the flat attachment.

In a pot, bring the sugar and water to a boil, and cook over medium heat for about 7 minutes, until the bubbles are smaller and the syrup is elastic—250°F (120°C) on a candy thermometer. Another way to test the consistency is to drip ½ teaspoon of the syrup into a cup of cold water—the syrup is ready when it turns into a gummy, elastic and clear ball between your fingers.

Turn on the mixer to medium speed, and carefully drizzle in the hot syrup, making sure it is poured against the side of the bowl. Add the vanilla, and mix for a few seconds, just until the syrup is completely incorporated into the raw tahini. Add the pistachios, and mix until they are evenly distributed in the mixture.

Spread the mixture in the prepared pan (work quickly because the halva starts to set instantly). Cover with a sheet of greased parchment paper, and set aside to cool.

Cut into cubes, and serve. Keep in a closed container at room temperature.

GRANDMA KNOWS BEST

You should have a candy thermometer for all the recipes that call for cooking sugar syrup to a precise temperature; it is a onetime investment that will guarantee the texture and success of any candy you make. With halva, for example, if the syrup is cooked to lower than 250°F (120°C), it will not crystalize and will remain very soft; if it is cooked to a higher temperature, it will be rock hard. However, if your halva is not at the perfect "noshing" consistency, don't throw it away—you can incorporate too-soft or too-hard halva crumbs into yeast roulades (sprinkle them over your favorite chocolate spread filling).

Turkish Delight

You don't have to wait for your next vacation to Turkey anymore—you can have your Turkish delight here and now. All you need to make it at home are two pots, a wire whisk and a little whisking forbearance. Traditionally, Turkish delight cubes are coated with powdered sugar (mixed with cornstarch to prevent soaking), but you can use desiccated coconut or chopped pistachios. Don't be afraid to play around with flavors either—use lemon zest, orange blossom water or any other natural flavor essence instead of the rose water.

ONE 12 X 8-INCH (30.5 X 20-CM) PAN OR 2 LOAF PANS

FOR THE SYRUP
4 cups (800g) granulated sugar
2 cups (480ml) water
Juice of ½ lemon

FOR THE CORNSTARCH MIXTURE
1 cup (140g) cornstarch
1 oz (28g) gelatin powder
2 cups (480ml) water
2 tbsp (30ml) rose water
1 tsp vinegar
A drop of red food coloring (optional)

FOR THE COATING
1 cup (120g) powdered sugar
1 cup (140g) cornstarch

Line a 12 x 8-inch (30.5 x 20-cm) baking pan or 2 loaf pans with parchment paper, and grease the paper.

To make the syrup, in a large pot (this is important!) over high heat, combine the granulated sugar and water and cook, stirring, until boiling. Turn the heat down, and let simmer without stirring for 10 minutes, until the mixture turns into a thick syrup. Add the lemon juice, and remove from the stove.

To make the cornstarch mixture, in another large pot (not yet on the stove), combine the cornstarch, gelatin, water, rose water and vinegar, and whisk thoroughly, until all lumps are smoothed out. Turn the heat on high, and bring to a boil while whisking. When bubbling starts, the mixture will become like porridge. Remove from the stove, carefully pour the mixture into the pot with the syrup and whisk until combined—there will be many lumps at first, but if you whisk vigorously, they will disappear. Cook for another 5 minutes over low heat, while stirring.

Remove from the heat (now is the time to add the food coloring if you want), and immediately pour the mixture into the prepared pan(s). Let cool to room temperature. Transfer the pans to the refrigerator for 4 hours to set.

To make the coating, combine the powdered sugar and cornstarch in a bowl. Spread the mixture generously on a cutting board. Release the edges of the candy from the pan with a knife, turn over onto the cutting board, and peel off the parchment paper. Sprinkle more powdered sugar and cornstarch mixture on top. With an oiled knife, cut into squares (carefully!). Roll the cubes in the dusting mixture so they are coated on all sides.

Serve immediately, or keep in a closed container at room temperature (in the summer, keep in the refrigerator).

GRANDMA KNOWS BEST
Here's a great tip for smooth and elegant slicing of this sticky delight: Spread some oil on the knife between slices. But promise to be extremely careful—a slippery work environment and a sharp knife are hazardous to the integrity of your fingers!

AND GRANDMA WOULD SAY
Stop gobbling down the Turkish delight! I need some to make cookies (see page 165).

Sesame Caramel Squares

To the time-honored recipe of these sesame squares, I add baking soda. Reacting with the honey's acidity, it makes the caramel more airy, so you don't break your teeth biting into it. Be very careful when you prepare this candy, and keep children (far) away—it is scalding hot!

ABOUT 40 SQUARES

2½ cups (400g) sesame seeds
1 tbsp (14g) margarine
1 cup (200g) sugar
½ cup (120ml) honey
½ tsp baking soda

Grease 2 sheets of parchment paper and set aside.

In a dry frying pan, toast the sesame seeds, stirring occasionally, until they are golden and fragrant. Set aside.

Melt the margarine in a wide pot (important—you can't mix everything in the frying pan). Add the sugar and honey and cook for 3–4 minutes over medium heat, stirring occasionally. The mixture will froth up, and that's okay. It is ready when the froth is caramel gold, and a nice caramel aroma fills the kitchen. Sprinkle over the baking soda, and mix immediately—it will rise and become a light orange froth with no liquid, and that's okay too. Add the toasted sesame seeds immediately, and patiently mix with a wooden spoon for about a minute, until the sesame seeds are all covered in caramel and sticky. Careful! It is extremely hot!!

Carefully pour the mixture onto one of the greased parchment sheets (did I mention it is very HOT?). Cover with the other parchment paper, greased side down, and flatten with a rolling pin to about ¼-inch (6-mm) thick.

Peel off the top parchment sheet, and cut with a long and smooth knife in any shape you like (just one downward motion with the knife, not a sawing motion). Set aside to cool for about ½ hour at room temperature, until it hardens. Break off individual sesame squares, and keep in a closed container on the counter.

GRANDMA KNOWS BEST

For diversity's sake, I like to add a handful of salted peanuts every once in a while. It goes well with the caramel's sweetness, and it breaks up the uniform look of the sesame seeds.

Luzina—Iraqi Quince Marmalade

An orange-colored sweet quince marmalade, coated in coconut flakes—to die for!

ONE 13 X 11-INCH (33 X 28-CM) PAN

5 large quinces (about 3¼ lb [1½kg])

Juice of 1 lemon

½ cup (120ml) water

5 cups (1kg) sugar

1 tsp ground cinnamon

About 2 cups (200g) desiccated coconut, divided, for coating

Put the quinces in a pot and fill with tap water to cover by about 1 inch (2.5cm). Bring to a boil over medium-high heat, and cook for 5 minutes. This partially softens the quinces, for easier peeling. Strain (no need to save the cooking water) and cool.

Peel and core the quinces. Grate in a food processor or on a grater, and immediately add the lemon juice to prevent discoloration.

Put the grated quince in the pot and add the water, sugar and cinnamon. Bring to a boil, reduce the heat to low and cook for about 1½ hours, stirring occasionally. The quinces will break down, dissolve and turn orange. The marmalade is ready when the mixture is thick and bright orange. To make sure, move the mixture in the pot with a spoon to reveal the bottom. It should take 1–2 seconds for the mixture to cover the exposed part again.

Line a 13 x 11-inch (33 x 28-cm) pan with parchment paper. Sprinkle 1 cup (100g) of the desiccated coconut over the paper in an even layer. Carefully spread the hot marmalade over the coconut. Sprinkle the remaining 1 cup (100g) coconut to cover the marmalade in the pan.

Leave overnight at room temperature to set (in the summer, keep in the refrigerator). Release from the pan, use the paper to help you, and cut into squares. Keep in a closed container at room temperature or in the refrigerator.

GRANDMA KNOWS BEST

Pectin is a natural gelling agent (a form of sugar) found in most fruit, mainly in their pits and skins. Quinces are rich in pectin, so they make a very firm marmalade. In confectionary shops, the chefs add pectin powder (available in specialty stores) to accelerate the gelling of fruit candies. In an acidic environment (hence the lemon juice) and heat, pectin powder turns a liquid to gel. The amount of powder varies according to the natural pectin content in each fruit (and in any case, it is only a teaspoon or so per pound [500g] of fruit). Pectin must be mixed with an equal amount of sugar before it is added to the pot to prevent lumps. If the jam you cooked is too runny, use pectin powder: Return the jam to the pot and bring to a boil. Add pectin powder (mixed with sugar), and cook for 5 minutes over low heat.

Candied Citrus Peels

The ultimate grandma candy—homemade candied orange peels. Making them at home comes with the wonderful bonus of the citrus aroma; the house smells like a citrus orchard in full bloom.

3 CUPS (300G)

FOR THE PEELS
2 qt (2L) water

2 tbsp (36g) coarse salt

Peels from 6 oranges (or 3 oranges and 2 grapefruits)

FOR THE SYRUP
4 cups (960ml) water

4 cups (800g) sugar

FOR COATING
About 1 cup (200g) sugar

To prepare the peels, in a bowl, combine the water and coarse salt. Add the citrus peels and let sit overnight at room temperature to take out the natural bitterness (see the "Grandma Knows Best" section below).

The next day, strain the peels, wash off the salt and put in a pot. Cover with fresh water and bring to a boil. Cook for about 30 minutes, until the peels have softened a little.

Strain the peels, and keep in the colander until the syrup is ready (use the pot you cooked the peels in for the syrup).

To make the syrup, in the same pot, combine the water and sugar and bring to a boil. Cook for 5 minutes, until the syrup thickens a little.

Add the citrus peels, and continue cooking over low heat until the peels are clear and glazed, 30–60 minutes depending on the thickness.

With tongs or a perforated spoon, remove the peels from the syrup and spread them on a parchment paper-lined baking sheet. Set aside for an hour to dry. If you like them really dry (they keep longer this way), dry them in an oven set on 250°F (120°C) for 30 minutes.

Cut the peels into strips, roll in the sugar to coat and serve. Keep in a closed container at room temperature.

GRANDMA KNOWS BEST
The overnight soaking in salt water neutralizes the bitterness of the inner white layer of the peel. It will not take out all the bitterness, but what is left is mild and nice. However, if you don't like this hint of bitterness, simply strain and repeat the soaking process for another 24 hours.

The Secret of Caramelized Pecans

Did you know you can make these at home? Caramelized pecans are cooked in syrup and then deep-fried (dietetic they are not). Homemade caramelized pecans are a lot crunchier than the store-bought ones, and much cheaper, too (especially if you can sweet-talk your neighbors into giving you some from the beautiful pecan tree growing in their garden).

3 CUPS (450G)

3 cups (600g) sugar

2 cups (480ml) water

3 cups (300g) peeled, untoasted pecans

Vegetable oil, for deep-frying

In a pot, heat the sugar and water over medium heat, stirring, until the sugar is dissolved. Add the pecans and bring to a boil. Lower the heat, and simmer for 10–15 minutes, until the nuts are shiny and have soaked up some syrup. Strain the nuts (the residual syrup is not necessary anymore).

In a pot, heat 3 inches (7.5cm) of oil to 350°F (180°C) on a deep-frying thermometer. Fry the nuts in small batches, until they turn dark brown, bringing the oil back up to temperature between batches. With a perforated spoon, take the nuts out of the oil, and put them in a colander or on a parchment paper–lined baking sheet (don't use paper towels, because they will stick to it). Let cool and enjoy. If—a big if—any are left, keep in a closed container at room temperature.

GRANDMA KNOWS BEST

It's not a good idea to put the nuts on a paper towel at any stage of the process, because they are very—very—sticky, and you won't be able to separate them from the paper towel. Yes, I tell you this from experience. Use a square of parchment paper instead.

Meringue Kisses

Forget everything you know about making a meringue. We are not going for the extreme caution approach with these nostalgic kisses—quite the opposite! What we need here is powerful action; the friction created by the long beating actually warms up the meringue, until it is like chewing gum—dense and shiny bright white. This means hard work for the mixer: 20 minutes of high-speed beating. That's right—20 minutes! Set the timer, and forget about the mixer until it buzzes you back. This is virtually impossible to achieve with a hand mixer, but any strong, modern professional countertop mixer is up to the task. After baking, you get dry, crunchy and hard kisses that crumble when you take a bite and melt in your mouth in a delightful cascade of sweetness.

50 LARGE "KISSES"

1 tsp vinegar
6 egg whites, at room temperature
2 cups (400g) sugar
A few drops of food coloring (optional)
Colored sprinkles (optional)

Make sure your mixer bowl and beating attachment are clean and dry. Pour the vinegar into the bowl, and with a piece of paper towel coat the entire inside of the bowl with it. If you don't have vinegar, rub the inside of the bowl with half a lemon.

Put the egg whites in the shiny mixer bowl, and beat at high speed for 1 minute, to get a soft white froth. Gradually add the sugar, while beating, 1 tablespoon (12g) at a time, with about a 5-second interval between spoonfuls. Beat for 20 minutes at high speed, until the meringue is white and shiny, very dense and has a "chewing gum" consistency (if your mixer heats up, let it rest for 5 minutes, and resume beating).

Preheat the oven to 225°F (110°C). Line a few baking sheets with parchment paper.

Stop the mixer. (Ah! Quiet at last!) If you choose to use food coloring, now is the time to add it (whether to the whole amount or just a part of it). Dip a toothpick in the food coloring, and dip it in the meringue (always add less than you think you need). Turn the mixer on low speed, and let it work just until the meringue is all colored. You can add some more if you want a darker result, but remember that the meringue goes darker during baking.

Put the meringue in a piping bag with a zigzag tip. You will have to do this in batches. Pipe kisses onto the prepared baking sheet (they can be piped close together, as they don't rise in the oven). If you want to use colored sprinkles, now is the time to sprinkle them on. They will stick nicely to the kisses.

Bake until completely dry, about 2½ hours. The kisses should remain light in color. If they start to turn gold, lower the oven's temperature to 200°F (100°C). When the kisses are done, they are easy to separate from the paper, and very light to the touch. Break one to make sure it is crispy and dry on the inside as well. Take out of the oven, and let cool completely. Keep in a closed container at room temperature.

GRANDMA KNOWS BEST

To make the kisses in two colors use a split piping bag, which you can find in specialty stores. You can't fit a piping tip in them, so prepare a large, regular piping bag with the tip of your choice, and insert the split piping bag in it. This way, you can also switch tips if you want to get different shapes of kisses. I used the 2D tips for the purple and turquoise kisses, and the 4B for the pink and white ones.

AND ANOTHER THING

Make sure the egg whites are cleanly separated, without a drop of yolk in them, and make very sure that the bowl is clean. I polish it with vinegar to neutralize any potential fat.

Krembo—Chocolate-Coated Marshmallow Treat (or "Warm Ice Cream")

Do you start eating your Krembo from the biscuit or from the chocolate? Having covered that key question, it's time to show you how to make it. The base is a short-crust pastry cookie, made soft and rich with egg yolks. The egg whites are beaten with a boiling sugar syrup that cooks them to a shiny meringue, which is piped over each cookie base. The whole thing is then coated with chocolate. Krembos are usually vanilla flavored, but you can flavor them any way you like (coffee—a teaspoon of instant coffee powder melted in a tablespoon [15 ml] of boiling water; banana—a few drops of natural banana essence, and so on). Flavoring is added to the egg whites toward the end of beating.

25 KREMBO

FOR THE COOKIES
1¼ cups (180g) all-purpose flour

1 tsp baking powder

¼ cup (50g) sugar

3½ oz (100g) cold butter, diced

3 egg yolks (save the whites for the meringue)

FOR THE MERINGUE
½ cup (120ml) water

1¼ cups (250g) sugar

3 egg whites

1 tsp vanilla extract

FOR COATING
11 oz (300g) dark chocolate

3 tbsp (45ml) vegetable oil

"HOT ICE CREAM"
Krembo's summery (and just as nostalgic) sister is a waffle cone filled with the Krembo meringue filling and covered with chocolate and colored sprinkles. The Krembo recipe makes 12 cones. Before you pipe the filling into the waffle cones, spoon in a little of the chocolate coating as a surprise. If you don't have a special holder for the cones, it is simple to construct one at home: wrap an empty loaf pan in aluminum foil, punch holes along the top (the open side) and insert the cones into the holes until just their tops show. Of course, you can choose the flat-base ice cream cones (less authentic but just as yummy).

Preheat the oven to 350°F (180°C). Line a baking sheet with parchment paper.

To make the cookies, in a food processor, combine the flour, baking powder, sugar and butter cubes, and mix to a crumbly consistency. Add the egg yolks, and mix in short pulses, just until the dough is homogenous and not sticky.

Roll the dough out on a sheet of parchment paper, until it is about ¼-inch (6-mm) thick. With a 2-inch (5-cm) fluted round cookie cutter, cut out 25 cookies (since only 25 cookies are needed for the Krembos, you can give any leftover dough to children to make their own cookies). Transfer to the prepared baking sheet.

Bake for 10–15 minutes, until golden. Let cool completely.

To make the meringue, in a small pot, bring the water and sugar to a boil over medium heat and cook, without stirring, until the syrup thickens and reaches 250°F (120°C) on a candy thermometer, about 7 minutes. Another way to test if it is at the desired temperature is to drip ½ teaspoon of the syrup into a cup of cold water—when it turns into a gummy and elastic ball in your fingers, it is ready.

Toward the end of cooking the syrup, begin beating the egg whites in a mixer at high speed. Beat for 2 minutes, until soft white froth forms.

Drizzle the syrup into the egg whites while beating at high speed (careful, it is HOT!). Beat for another 5 minutes, until the mixer bowl is warm, but not too hot to the touch. Add the vanilla, and beat for a few more seconds, until combined.

Put the meringue into a piping bag with a smooth, ½-inch (1.3-cm) wide tip, and pipe a plump hill of it onto each cookie. Put in the freezer for 20 minutes to set.

To make the coating, in a microwave-safe bowl, melt the chocolate in a microwave oven. Add the oil, and mix to combine. Pour into a tall narrow container, and let cool to room temperature.

Hold each Krembo by its cookie and turn it upside down into the chocolate coating.

Return to the freezer for 5 minutes for the coating to set. Keep in the refrigerator, and serve cold.

White Nougat with Almonds and Peanuts

My grandparents lived in suburban Haifa. To visit us, they would take a bus up to the Ron Movie Theater, where we would pick them up with my mom's old Simca-1000. While waiting, my sister and I would drag our mother to the nearby candy stand—close to the Talpiot Market. Dana would choose the bright yellow banana candies, Mom would always buy the chocolate-coated half-moon cookies and I invariably asked for the cellophane-wrapped nougat. I know now that the beloved white candy, also called "nougat de Montélimar" or "torrone," is really easy to make at home. You make an egg white meringue with a lot of hot honey syrup (which cooks the egg whites, so don't worry). This is easy on the chef, but quite an undertaking for the mixer, so don't try to make it with a hand mixer—use the countertop professional type (it too shall struggle a little, and be slower than usual). The nougat must be sent to the freezer for 2 hours to set. It will not be hard, but maintain a delightful chewing-gum consistency. You can dip each slice into melted chocolate (and don't miss out on my version of the Egozi candy bar on page 225).

20 BARS

FOR THE SYRUP
2 cups (400g) sugar
½ cup (120ml) honey
¼ cup (60ml) water

FOR THE MERINGUE
2 egg whites
¼ tsp salt

FOR THE ADD-INS
1 cup (100g) peeled, toasted and unsalted almonds
1 cup (100g) peeled, toasted and unsalted peanuts

Line a loaf pan with a sheet of parchment paper, and generously grease the paper. Prepare another sheet of greased parchment paper to cover the candy later. Set aside

To make the syrup, in a pot over medium heat, heat the sugar, honey and water, stirring, until the sugar is completely dissolved. Bring to a boil, and cook over medium heat for about 5 minutes. Initially, there will be a lot of white foam over the syrup, which will gradually go down until almost all of it will disappear, and the syrup will turn deep gold with little bubbles (270°F [130°C] on a candy thermometer). The sweet honey aroma that fills the kitchen is a nice bonus. Another way to test if the syrup has the desired consistency is to drip ½ teaspoon of it into a cup of cold water—if it hardens into a rubbery, hard ball that can be squeezed between your fingers, it is ready.

When the syrup is almost completely cooked, make the meringue. In a mixer, beat the egg whites and salt at medium speed into a soft white froth.

Carefully (it's very HOT!) pour the syrup into the egg whites while beating. Go on beating at medium speed for about 5 minutes, until the mixer bowl is warm but not too hot to the touch. The mixture will be gummy and sticky, which will slow down the mixer.

For the add-ins, with an oiled spatula (preferably one with a long, sturdy handle), fold in the almonds and peanuts. Immediately transfer the mixture to the prepared pan. Cover with the greased sheet of parchment paper, and press down with your hands to get an even layer. Put in the freezer for 2 hours to set.

Turn the nougat out of the pan. Peel off the two sheets (top and bottom) of parchment paper, and cut into rectangles of the desired size (oil the knife if necessary, to prevent sticking). Serve immediately. Keep covered in the refrigerator.

GRANDMA KNOWS BEST

When confectionary chefs refer to "nougat," they mean hazelnut paste (the spiritual ancestor of Nutella). The French, however, call it nougat de Montélimar, named after its Provence origins. I call it "white nougat," so I won't be confused. In the original recipe, the nougat is prepared between two store-bought wafer (or rice) sheets, to prevent sticking. I prefer it without any underlying flavor, so I prepare it in a loaf pan lined with greased parchment paper.

AND ANOTHER THING

For this recipe, I strongly recommend a candy thermometer, because if you heat the syrup over 270°F (130°C), the candy will be too hard for slicing and for eating, and if you fail to reach 270°F (130°C), it will be a little runny.

Egozi Bar

Egozi comes from the Hebrew word for "nuts," which this candy bar is full of. A picture is worth a thousand words, right? As a sworn Egozi fanatic since childhood, I just had to include a homemade version of it in this book, which is all about nostalgia. This is hands down the most decadent to-die-for recipe in the entire book. Preparation is intricate and challenging, but if you brave it, the result will definitely justify the effort.

FORTY 1 X 3-INCH (2.5 X 7.5-CM) BARS

FOR THE CHOCOLATE BASE AND COATING
11 oz (300g) milk chocolate
2 tbsp (40g) Nutella
1 tbsp (15ml) vegetable oil

FOR THE HAZELNUTS
2 cups (200g) hazelnuts

FOR THE WHITE NOUGAT
2 cups (400g) granulated sugar
½ cup (120ml) honey
¼ cup (60ml) water
2 egg whites
A pinch of salt

FOR THE TOFFEE
3½ oz (100g) butter, diced
1 (14 oz [400g]) can condensed milk
2 tbsp (40g) honey
¾ cup (180g) dark brown sugar

Line a 13 x 11-inch (33 x 28-cm) rectangular pan with a sheet of parchment paper and grease the paper. Set aside.

To make the chocolate base, in a microwave oven, melt the milk chocolate. Stir in the Nutella and oil. Reserve half of the mixture for coating. With the back of a spoon, spread the other half of the mixture in an even layer on the bottom of the pan. Keep in the freezer until assembly (at least for 10–20 minutes).

To prepare the hazelnuts, preheat the oven to 350°F (180°C). Line a baking sheet with parchment paper. Spread the nuts in the pan, in one layer, and toast them for 10 minutes, until the thin brown skin cracks. Let cool a little, and rub them with your hands—a handful at a time—until all the skin falls off. Get rid of the skin, and set the peeled nuts aside for later.

To make the nougat, in a large pot (this is important, because the mixture rises when boiled!) over medium heat, combine the granulated sugar, honey and water, stirring, until the sugar is completely dissolved. Bring to a boil, lower the heat to medium and cook for about 5 minutes, until the froth disappears and the syrup is thick and deep gold and there are little bubbles (270°F [130°C] on a candy thermometer). Toward the end of the syrup's cooking time, in a mixer, beat the egg whites and salt at medium speed until a soft white froth forms. Carefully (it's very HOT!) pour the syrup into the egg whites, while beating. Continue beating at medium speed for 5 minutes, until the bowl is only slightly warm (don't be alarmed when the mixer slows down, because the meringue is very thick at this point). Add the nuts, and fold them in with a spatula, working quickly, because the nougat starts setting right away. Immediately pour the mixture over the chocolate layer in the pan, spreading it with a wet or oiled spatula to prevent sticking. Return to the freezer to set, 10–20 minutes.

To make the toffee, in a large pot (this is important, because the mixture rises when boiled!), heat the butter, condensed milk, honey and brown sugar over low heat, stirring occasionally, until all the sugar is dissolved. Turn up the heat to medium, and bring to a boil. Boil for 5 minutes, stirring occasionally, until the mixture is so thick the bubbles can't pop on the surface and it looks like a boiling swamp (250°F [120°C] on a candy thermometer). Remove from the stove, and let cool for 5 minutes (an absolute must—or the hot toffee will melt the nougat!). Pour an even layer of toffee over the nougat (don't scrape the bottom of the pot, because what is stuck there is invariably burnt and a little bitter). Return it to the freezer for 10–20 minutes to set.

In a microwave oven, heat the remaining chocolate mixture a little. Gently spread it over the toffee layer until covered. Put in the freezer for 2 hours to set. Release the candy from the pan by pulling the parchment paper. Cut and serve cold.

Easy-Peasy Chocolate Balls

Even in the fanciest pastry shops, featuring the most intricate and alluring cakes, I ask for a chocolate ball (and I devour it in the car, so I will not be made fun of when I get home). Chocolate balls bring an instant smile to my face, and I think they are better than many other, fancier desserts. Here are two wonderful recipes. Unable to decide which to include and which to exclude, I give you both; one for the balls (an easy Nutella, whipping cream and Petit-Beurre recipe) and the other for an addictive chocolate "sausage" (the classic version, upgraded with chocolate).

25 BALLS

9 oz (250g) Petit-Beurre biscuits

1 cup (240ml) whipping cream

1 cup (320g) Nutella

Desiccated coconut or colored sprinkles, for the coating (optional)

Break the biscuits into little pieces (I like to bash them in a plastic bag with a rolling pin).

In a pot over medium heat, bring the whipping cream to near boiling, remove from the heat and mix in the Nutella. Add the biscuit crumbs, and mix well. Cover and put in the refrigerator for 2–3 hours (or ½ hour in the freezer) to set.

Roll the mixture into balls (wet your hands if they are sticky). Roll each ball in desiccated coconut or colored sprinkles, place in paper liners and keep in the refrigerator until you are ready to serve.

Chocolate and Biscuit "Sausage"

Chocolate balls, chocolate sausage—it is merely a matter of design. You can make the sausage with the previous recipe, but I also share another superb version, reminiscent of the classic chocolate balls traditionally made with cocoa powder. This one is upgraded with dark chocolate (and lots of it!).

30 PIECES

9 oz (250g) Petit-Beurre biscuits

¾ cup (180ml) milk

3 tbsp (40g) granulated sugar

3½ oz (100g) butter, diced

7 oz (200g) dark chocolate, broken into pieces

Powdered sugar or ground Lotus biscuits, for coating

Break the biscuits into little pieces (I like to bash them in a plastic bag with the rolling pin).

In a pot over medium heat, heat the milk and granulated sugar, stirring, until the sugar is dissolved (don't let it boil). Add the butter and chocolate, and heat, stirring, until they melt. Remove from the stove. Add the biscuit crumbs, and mix well. Let cool a little.

With wet hands, roll into 2 cylinders.

Roll the cylinders in powdered sugar or Lotus crumbs, and freeze for 1 hour to set. Slice each sausage into 15 coins and serve. Keep in the refrigerator.

GRANDMA KNOWS BEST

For diversity (or if you are just too lazy to roll and shape), simply spread the hot mixture in a greased disposable loaf pan, spread with the coating of your choice, and freeze for 1 hour to set. Slice and serve.

Choco-Pie—the Home Tribute

Burger Ranch is an Israeli burger chain, and its Choco-Pie was the dessert (with a capital D) of my youth. Whenever we ate there, my dessert would wait in the famous red container until I finished off my favorite (hot and spicy) burger. All grown up, I bought it again, tasted it and was successful in re-creating it at home. It's quite simple, actually—you take a crepe (store-bought), fill it with chocolate-flavored pudding, coat in egg and crumbs (like a schnitzel) and deep-fry. There is only one thing about the old-days Choco-Pie that I don't miss—the burned tongue—so wait a few minutes before you eat it: the chocolate filling is scolding hot!

15 CHOCO-PIES

FOR THE CHOCOLATE CRÈME PÂTISSIÈRE FILLING

2 cups (480ml) milk, divided

6 egg yolks

¼ cup (40g) cornstarch

¾ cup (150g) granulated sugar

5½ oz (150g) dark chocolate

FOR THE BLINTZES (CREPES)

15 blintzes, store-bought or homemade (page 188)

Vegetable oil, for deep-frying

FOR THE COATING

¾ cup (100g) powdered sugar

2 eggs, whisked

2 tbsp (30ml) milk

2 cups (200g) breadcrumbs

To make the chocolate crème pâtissière, in a bowl, combine ½ cup (120ml) of the milk, egg yolks and cornstarch. Whisk until the mixture is homogenous and lump-free.

In a pot, bring the remaining 1½ cups (360ml) milk and the granulated sugar to a near boil. Remove from the stove, and drizzle one-third of the hot milk mixture into the yolk mixture, while whisking.

Transfer the yolk mixture to the pot with the remaining hot milk, and heat over medium heat, whisking constantly, bringing it again to a near boil (the cream will become very thick). At the first bubbling, remove from the stove. Add the chocolate, and stir until dissolved.

Transfer it to the mixer fitted with the flat attachment, and let cool. Mix at medium speed for 10 minutes, until the cream is at room temperature.

To prepare the blintzes, place a blintz (crepe) on your work surface, take a heaping spoon of the cold cream and spread it in a line across the crepe. Fold the sides of the crepe toward the center (so the cream will not ooze out), and roll like a spring roll. Toward the end of rolling, brush the edge with a little whisked egg (which you "steal" from the eggs prepared for the coating) and tighten it shut, so the crepe will not open when fried. Put the filled blintzes on a tray, and freeze for 1 hour, to partially harden, which makes coating and frying easier.

In a pot, heat 3 inches (7.5cm) of oil to 350°F (180°C) on a deep-frying thermometer.

To prepare the coating, fill 3 flat bowls, one with the powdered sugar, one with the eggs and milk (whisked until combined) and one with breadcrumbs. Roll each blintz in the powdered sugar, then in the egg mixture and finally in the breadcrumbs.

Deep-fry a few at a time, being careful not to crowd the pot, until golden. Remove with a slotted spoon or spider and put on a paper towel to absorb the excess oil. Cool a little before serving (the filling is HOT!). You can do everything except the frying a day in advance, just cover the filled and coated blintzes, keep them in the refrigerator and fry before serving.

GRANDMA KNOWS BEST

Too lazy to prepare the chocolate crème pâtissière? Here is a brilliant and quick alternative: Prepare chocolate-flavored Jell-O mix according to the box (you'll need 4 cups of the pudding for the entire recipe). Once set, whisk until smooth and use to fill the blintzes.

WHO IS THIS LITTLE BUNDLE OF SWEETNESS?

Check out this cutie pie! That's Adam, my sweet nephew (my sister Dana's son), the one from the ma'amouls on page 145.

About the Author

CARINE GOREN is a self-taught baker and recipe developer. She has written several bestselling books, each geared toward simplifying the baking process for the home cook. She is a popular TV host in Israel and has 250,000 Facebook followers. "Carine Goren" was the most Googled person in Israel in 2015, and her recipes are often the most sought-after by home bakers. Goren is also a judge in the Israeli version of the reality show *Bake Off.*

The Israeli baking guru is now coming to the United States with one of her most successful cookbooks, *Traditional Jewish Baking*, so get ready to fall in love with your grandmother's recipes all over again.

Born in 1974, Goren is married to her high school sweetheart and lives in a small village near Tel Aviv.

Index